Parkland Palate

Compiled by

Anne (Nesbitt) Mense

In 1985 Canada celebrates the Centennial of National Parks. Across the nation people from all walks of life are exercising creativity and expending energy on projects that reflect their personal interest in and relationships with Canada's national parks. This collection of regional recipes, laced with personal descriptions and anecdotes of national parks in the many corners of Canada is one such project. It displays the grass-roots concern for Canada's heritage — in this case both natural and culinary — that is the real driving force behind the success of the national parks.

P. A. Thomson
Director
National Parks Research

National Parks Centennial

1885

1985

Centenaire des parcs nationaux

1885–1985:
100 years of Heritage Conservation
Canada's first national park was established in 1885 at Banff, Alberta. Today there are national parks and national historic parks in every province and territory. The National Parks Centennial is an occasion to renew our commitment to preserve examples of our heritage unimpaired for the benefit of all Canadians.

Parkland Palate

Compiled by
Anne (Nesbitt) Mense

First Printing — September, 1984

Copyright © 1984 by
ARK PUBLISHING
697 Patricia Avenue
Winnipeg, Manitoba
R3T 3A8

Canadian Cataloguing in Publication Data

Mense, Anne, 1951-
  Parkland palate

Includes index.
ISBN 0-919845-15-0

1. Cookery, Canadian. 2. National parks
and reserves — Canada. I. Title.
TX715.M45 1984   641.5971   C84-
091463-6

Photography by:

Lance Thomson
Display Photographic
Winnipeg, Manitoba.

Design by Cynthia Del Rosso

Designed, Printed, and Produced in
Canada by

Centax of Canada
1048 Fleury Street
Regina, Saskatchewan, Canada S4N 4W8

#105-4711 13 Street N.E.
Calgary, Alberta, Canada T2E 6M3

Introduction

This book began as a simple collection of recipes to commemorate the National Parks of Canada Centennial in 1985. But, somewhere along the way, this menagerie of memory and experience began to independently chart its own unique course!

The inspiration for this project came from two sources. Firstly, it came from a group of women in Riding Mountain National Park who faithfully met every summer to exchange their most treasured recipes, to taste their new inventions, and to share experiences of the past year. During the long cold prairie winters they often took refuge in their warm kitchens and baked some of these recipes, a reminder of close friends and sunny, lazy, summer days.

The other source of inspiration was the Riding Mountain National Park 50th Anniversary Committee. This industrious group planned and organized some marvelous activities for the park's 50th Anniversary. Plans are under way for Centennial Celebrations and my children and I are awaiting the festivities with anxious anticipation!

In the aftermath of last summer's excitement, it occurred to me that one way to commemorate the Centennial might be the compilation of a National Parks cookbook so that people from all across the country could share the Centennial spirit! I began to collect recipes from people who were connected with all of the National Parks.

As the book progressed, I found that I was gathering other things as well and the project was emerging quite differently than I had envisioned. As well as recipes, it became an accumulation of slides, illustrations, and stories. The anecdotes recounted episodes from recent years, from the past and to my surprise — some of the stories even went back millions of years!

I think this assemblage has barely scratched the surface. However, I hope that you will enjoy sharing this collection and that it will revive memories and promote shared experiences during your Centennial Celebrations!

As for me — I am heading off to visit some of the parks that I haven't been to as yet and I am hoping to meet some of the people whose recipes are now a part of our family's life!

Anne

(Nesbitt) Mense

Acknowledgements

This whole book is, in many ways, a thank you. However, we would like to specifically thank everyone who submitted recipes. Unfortunately, we could not include all of the recipes but we have chosen a representative selection.

This book would not be possible without the skillful organization and editing of Kathie Anderson.

There are also some other people who made significant contributions: Rea Nesbitt — recipe testing, Sheila Murphy — recipe testing, Lynne Dumesnil — translations.

Expertise and information was provided by: Celes Davar, Janelle Reynolds, Cathy Aubin, Bernie Lieff, Merna Forster, Ken Walker, W. J. Masyk, Jeff Thompson, Merv Syroteuk, Daniel Weedon, Michael Jones, Denise Jordan, L. Meleg, Keith Dewar, C. Bédard, Barry F. Spencer, A. A. MacLean, Peter Hope, Robert G. McNeil, Bill Fisher, G. F. Robert Lohnes, G. Marsh, J. L. Feick.

Illustrations were supplied by:
Pacific Rim National Park — on pages: 88, 90
Riding Mountain National Park — on pages: 10, 14, 24, 28
Prince Albert National Park — on page: 160
Prince Edward Island National Park — on pages: 27, 30, 32, 44, 78, 86
Rick Swain — Kejimkujik National Park — on pages: 23, 34, 39, 158
Gaileen Marsh — Terra Nova National Park — on pages: 47, 66, 126, 128
Bente Cunnings — on pages: 18, 33, 54, 101, 108
D. Verhalle — Riding Mountain National Park — on page: 10

Slides are courtesy of:
Pacific Rim National Park
Waterton Lakes National Park
Prince Albert National Park
Parks Canada Prairie Region

We received kind and generous co-operation from Parks Canada.

The National Parks of Canada preserve the rare gift of nature and history for us and for future generations. Although, some of the recipes contained in this collection incorporate wild plants and wildlife, these have been included mainly for their historical significance. We are convinced that our readers will respect and support the National Park endeavours and will not disturb their natural environments.

Canada's National Parks

It all starts 100 years ago! Or does it? Certainly the National Park system, as we know it, starts with the establishment of Banff National Park in 1885. Now, National Parks and National Historic Parks are established in every province and territory. In 1985 the National Parks celebrate their Centennial. This is an occasion to renew our commitment to preserve examples of our heritage, unimpaired for the benefit of all Canadians. It is also a time to enjoy and appreciate the wonderful benefits that we derive from our extensive park system.

What are the National Parks? This is the question that confronts me as I investigate the Centennial. In search of an answer, I begin by reading countless pamphlets, articles, and books about our National Parks. Through all the facts and figures I discover that our National Parks contain some of the most spectacular and challenging geography in the world. This is important, but it certainly seems to be missing something as far as I am concerned. So, I take a step further.

I begin to investigate park policy. I am sure that most Canadians have some sense that the National Parks are tracts of land that are set aside to preserve our outstanding natural areas for present and future generations to enjoy. However, the National Parks go a step further. They are dedicated to the people of Canada. The Parks provide us with the priceless gifts of enjoyment and recreation. They encourage public education through their varied and interesting interpretive programs. The National Parks promote scientific research and investigation. Park atmospheres provide inspiration for the wealth of creative talent that flourishes in Canada. The National Historic Parks provide the vital function of preserving our history and national identity.

As I explore these various aspects of the National Parks, I begin to feel a pervasive sense that the most important function of our parks is to guide us back to an intrinsic relationship which is sadly ignored in modern society. I discover that, throughout the ages, man insures his survival by cultivating a sensitivity and a respectful reverence for nature. He lives in harmony with the land and with wildlife because his existence depends upon it. These days, our sensibility to our fragile natural purlieu is numbed by the harshness of concrete and plastic. We are neglectfully detached from our true essence and forget that our lives still depend on the delicate balance that must be maintained with our natural surroundings. The National Parks serve as a beacon, enticing us to re-establish that essential relationship with our natural environment which could prove to be the key to our survival.

Even though all these purposes are crucial, I still have the nagging feeling that, in my experience, the National Parks mean something more. So I decide to explore my own relationship with the National Parks.

For me, my conception of the National Parks is specifically related to one park — Riding Mountain National Park. My relationship with this park begins even before my birth. Its origins go back to my grandparents, who have been going to Clear Lake for over 50 years. For my Grandfather, at 91, the summer at Riding Mountain National Park is still the highlight of his year! This tradition is passed down to me through my parents and is now continued to my children — who, like their great-grandfather, count the days until they can enjoy the summer at Clear Lake. We are by no means extraordinary in this, because there are countless families across Canada whose generations share a commitment to particular National Parks.

To me, Riding Mountain National Park means — FAMILY. No matter where our lives take us throughout the year, we all make a special effort to congregate during the summer months at Clear Lake. This is the time when birthdays are celebrated, memories are shared, friendships are rekindled, and futures are planned. As in many families across Canada, it is a time for visitors. The guest books across the country can attest to the procession of visiting relatives and friends who share summer fun with countless families in the National Parks.

During my younger days, my camping experiences in and near the park helped me develop working relationships with others. These experiences provided me with opportunities to discover who I was and what I wanted in life. As they have done for many young people, the National Parks provided the environment which helped me to develop the foundations of my life.

Like many young people each year, I enjoyed summer employment in the park, which helped me to finance my university education. During these student years, The National Parks also provided inexpensive vacations. These vacations were some of the most memorable!

The parks, for me, are a place where it is possible to get in touch with our heritage. This may be in terms of our own family connections, however, it may extend much further. The National Park system, which includes National Historic Parks, offers us the opportunity to explore our relationship with our country, our customs, and our heritage. This journey can lead us back 50 years, 100 years or even to the beginning of time!

Riding Mountain National Park is also a setting, within which, I can explore my relationship with nature and with the universe. For me, as well as for many others, this natural setting is the inspiration for my creative expression. Most of my weavings and fibre pieces are created from images of wildlife or experiences in Riding Mountain National Park that capture my imagination.

The Park, on many occasions, is a refuge. This retreat is where I often return when I am working through life's problems. Most of the major decisions in my life are made in the quiet peace of the park. From the strength of that environment, I face the frustration of turmoil and the helplessness of grief as so many before me have done.

For me, and for countless others in these times of transition, the parks provide stability. Homes may change, friends change, jobs change, life changes. But, in the midst of all this, you can return each year, to a place you have known since childhood. Although cosmetic appearances are altered occasionally, the park basically remains the same, providing the anchor which helps you weather the fluctuations in your life.

In my search for what the National Parks really are, I find that they are much more than "just" beautiful scenery and spectacular geography. Their purpose goes much deeper than conservation and preservation. For a truer sense of what the National Parks are, maybe we have to think in terms of an intricate system of relationships. Each of the 29 National Parks offers its own unique experiences to Canadians. Since everyone develops their own relationship with the various National parks, the possibilities are endless! There is a special system of complex feelings that each of us has for the National Parks. For me, the National Parks mean — HOME! What do they mean for you?

1. **Pacific Rim National Park** — 1970
2. **Mount Revelstoke National Park** — 1914
3. **Glacier National Park** — 1886
4. **Yoho National Park** — 1886
5. **Kootenay National Park** — 1920
6. **Waterton Lakes National Park** — 1895
7. **Banff National Park** — 1885
8. **Jasper National Park** — 1907
9. **Elk Island National Park** — 1913
10. **Kluane National Park** — 1972
11. **Nahanni National Park** — 1972
12. **Wood Buffalo National Park** — 1922
13. **Prince Albert National Park** — 1927
14. **Riding Mountain National Park** — 1929
15. **Pukaskwa National Park** — 1971
16. **Georgian Bay Islands National Park** — 1929
17. **Point Pelee National Park** — 1918
18. **St. Lawrence Islands National Park** — 1904
19. **La Mauricie National Park** — 1970
20. **Auyuittuq National Park Reserve** — 1972
21. **Forillon National Park** — 1970
22. **Kouchibouguac National Park** — 1969
23. **Fundy National Park** — 1947
24. **Prince Edward Island National Park** — 1937
25. **Kejimkujik National Park** — 1968
26. **Cape Breton Highlands National Park** — 1936
27. **Gros Morne National Park** — 1970
28. **Terra Nova National Park** — 1957
29. **Grasslands National Park** — 1981

Note: The dates after each national park are the dates when that particular park
　　　was established as a national park.

8

TABLE
OF
CONTENTS

All recipes in this cookbook have been tested in both imperial and metric.

Riding Mountain National Park

North Gate

Moon Lake

#10 Parkway

Lake Audy

Lake Audy Road

Clear Lake

Wasagaming

Whirlpool Lake

Highway #19

East Gate

BEVERAGES & APPETIZERS

Lake O'Hara Hot Cider

10-12 oz.	bottles dry cider	10 - 341 mL
1¼ cups	brown sugar	300 mL
1½ tsp.	cinnamon	7 mL
1½ tsp.	cloves	7 mL
½ tsp.	allspice	2 mL
4 tbsp.	Triple Sec	60 mL
2 cups	dark rum	500 mL
1 cup	brandy	250 mL
	orange and lemon slices	

Bring the cider to a boil and add the brown sugar. When the sugar dissolves, add the remaining ingredients. Serve hot. Garnish with orange and lemon slices. Serves 20.

Lake O'Hara Lodge
Banff, Alta.

Banff
National Park

Percolator Hot Punch

3 - 48 oz.	cans apple juice	4 - 1.36 L
4 cups	cranberry cocktail	1 L
½ cup	brown sugar	125 mL
½ tsp.	salt	2 mL
4	cinnamon sticks	4
4	whole cloves	4

In a 30-40 cup (8 - 10 L) percolator, combine apple juice and cranberry cocktail. Combine sugar, salt, cinnamon sticks, and cloves in the percolator basket.

Plug in, and percolate as you would for coffee. When serving, pour a small amount of rum into a cup, and add hot punch.

This is a welcome treat after a few hours of cross-country skiing! Yields 22 cups (5.5 L).

Joy Lieff
Waterton Park, Alta.

Waterton Lakes
National Park

Anniversary Punch

2 - 48 oz.	cans orange juice	1.36 L
48 oz.	can pineapple juice	1.36 L
64 oz.	cranberry cocktail	1.82 L
4 - 32 oz.	bottles 7 up	1 L
½	bag of ice	½

Combine all ingredients and serve. The juices can be mixed ahead of time, and the 7 up and ice added just before serving if desired.

Sometimes we add lemon juice, grenadine, fresh strawberries, pineapple chunks, mandarin orange segments, or vodka. Yields 22 cups (5.5 L).

50th Anniversary Committee　　　　　　　　　　*Riding Mountain*
Clear Lake, Man.　　　　　　　　　　　　　　*National Park*

The 50th Anniversary Committee was established to organize and co-ordinate events celebrating the 50th Anniversary of Riding Mountain National Park. They brought groups such as the Treble Teen Singers and the Dugald Ladies Fashion Show to the park. They organized parades, band concerts, sing songs, talent shows, Pioneer Days, and many other activities during the summer. Their tireless efforts made it a summer to remember!

Anniversary Punch became a standard item at many of the activities. They served it "spiked" for the Craft Show Reception. The Shriners thought it was spiked. The Treble Teens wished it was spiked. After the Grand Parade, they didn't care whether or not it was spiked, and at the wind-up party, they needed it spiked!

See photograph page 48.

Summer Slush

3 cups	sugar	750 mL
3 cups	water	750 mL
14 oz.	can pineapple chunks and juice	398 mL
9 oz.	jar maraschino cherries and juice	250 mL
1	grapefruit	1
3	lemons	3
3	oranges	3

Combine sugar and water in a large saucepan. Stir over medium heat until sugar is dissolved. Cool. Add pineapple and cherries.

Peel grapefruit, lemons, and oranges and cut into small pieces. Add to the sugar/water mixture. Pour into plastic yogurt or margarine containers, and freeze.

To serve, remove from freezer about 5-10 minutes before serving. It should be served slushy. Don't take it out of the freezer too soon, as it melts quickly. Yields 6-8 cups (1.5-2 L).

Marion Brunsoman
Fountain Hills, Arizona

Riding Mountain
National Park

See photograph page 16.

Banana Slush

2 cups	sugar	500 mL
6 cups	water	1.5 L
12½ oz.	frozen lemon juice concentrate	355 mL
12½ oz.	frozen orange juice concentrate	355 mL
48 oz.	can pineapple juice	1.36 L
5	bananas, mashed	5
	7 up	

Combine sugar and water in a large saucepan, and stir over medium heat until sugar is dissolved. Cool.

Add lemon juice, orange juice, pineapple juice, and bananas. Mix well. Pour into plastic yogurt or margarine containers, and freeze.

To serve, allow mixture to thaw a few minutes — just until it becomes slushy. Don't leave it out too long! Pour ⅓ cup (75 mL) in a glass, and add 7 up. Makes about 32 servings.

Lorraine Schmidt
Waskesiu Lake, Sask.

Prince Albert
National Park

Yogurt Smoothie

1 cup	yogurt	250 mL
2 tsp.	sugar substitute	10 mL
1	frozen banana	1
⅛ tsp.	nutmeg or vanilla	0.5 mL
½ cup	crushed ice	125 mL

Combine all ingredients in a blender, and process until thick and creamy.

Variation: Use any other frozen unsweetened fruit. Add 1 egg or 1 tbsp. (15 mL) bran if desired. Serves 1.

Rachel Herchak-Gendron
Onanole, Man.

Riding Mountain
National Park

See photograph page 128.

Chocolate Eggnog

8 cups	eggnog	2 L
¼ cup	chocolate syrup	50 mL
¾ cup	rum	175 mL
1½ cups	whipping cream	375 mL
3 tbsp.	sugar	45 mL
1 tbsp.	cocoa	15 mL
½ oz.	semisweet chocolate	15 g

Combine eggnog, syrup, and rum. Beat with the mixmaster on high to blend well. Pour into punch bowl.

Whip cream, sugar, and cocoa until still. Spoon onto eggnog. Sprinkle with shaved semisweet chocolate. Serves 10 - 12.

Joy Lieff
Waterton Park Alta.

Waterton Lakes
National Park

Clear Lake Coffee

1 oz.	rum	25 mL
½ oz.	Tia Maria	15 mL
1 cup	hot coffee	250 mL
	vanilla ice cream	

Add the rum and Tia Maria to a cup of hot coffee. Top with ice cream. This is great around the campfire. Serves 1.

Bev Gowler
Winnipeg, Man.

Riding Mountain
National Park

One of the evening attractions in Riding Mountain National Park is the Park Theatre. It is the largest log theatre on the North American continent. This unique theatre was built through a make-work construction project during the depression and was completed in 1939.

Pacific Rim National Park

British Columbia

Pacific Rim National Park reflects the irony in the name Pacific Ocean. Although this ocean often has a peaceful appearance, as on the day Balboa first named it, you have only to stand on Long Beach, mesmerized by the gigantic waves thundering to shore, to realize the harsh brutality of its presence.

It is, in fact, this treacherousness that predominates the history of this coast. Over 40 ships have met their demise on the rugged shoreline of this "Graveyard of the Pacific". In 1906 the passenger ship S.S. Valentina was battered and crushed by the relentless seas. One hundred and twenty-six people perished as would-be rescuers watched impotently. The next year the federal government began constructing a lighthouse at Pachena Point. The West Coast Trail was also established, linking lighthouses and towns along the coast, so that shipwrecked sailors could reach the safety of coastal communities. With the advent of modern navigation and communications, the trail fell into disuse. However, this historic trail has recently been revived as a hiking trail which demands stamina and hiking expertise.

The immense unpredictibility of the ocean extends to the Broken Islands Group. There are about 100 islands in this cluster which are accessible only by boat. The outermost islands are fully exposed to the writhing force of the Pacific Ocean but, behind these outer islands, protected waterways provide more tranquil conditions.

In contrast to the harshness which sometimes occurs, is the awesome serenity you can experience as you lie in your tent listening to the Gray Whales gracefully swashing by. Peacefulness also pervades as you scuba dive near playful sea lions or tangle with a friendly octopus. New worlds open as you watch barnacles, mussels, anenome, and hermit crabs in quiescent tidal pools and sea caves.

Silent stillness encompasses the rain forest where time seems to stand still. The forest looks much the same as it did 10 centuries ago. The character of this forest endures because constant winter rain and summer fog keeps fires in check, naturally preserving one of the oldest forests on earth. For thousands of years this forest has serenely continued its cycle of decay and rebirth.

Thus, our first national marine park conserves the contrast between a harsh unpredictable ocean and a peaceful immutable land.

Chokecherry Vinegar:
A Bellevue House Cordial

10 lbs	chokecherries	5 kg
2½ qts.	vinegar	2.5L
10 lbs.	white sugar	5 kg

Put the chokecherries through a food chopper to break the pits. Add the vinegar to the fruit and let stand for 4 or 5 days, stirring occasionally. Put through a strainer and add sugar to the liquid. If you like it rather acid, reduce the quantity of sugar. Boil for ½ hour. To serve, dilute with water to taste. Yields approximately 15 - 20 servings.

Kingston, Ont.

Bellevue House
National Historic Park

This recipe dates from the 1840's and is served on special occasions at Bellevue House. It was in the possession of the gardener at Bellevue House, Mr. Russell Ferguson, and was passed down to him by his grandmother.

Bellevue House was built between 1838 and 1840, by Charles Hales. He was a grocer and so the house at that time was nicknamed "Tea Caddy Castle". During John A. Macdonald's brief stay in the house, his family named it "Bellevue" because of the breathtaking view from its tower. The name is somewhat ironic because their stay in the house was far from happy. Their infant son died, Macdonald's wife was ill, and they were plagued with financial worries.

Champagne Gaspésien

4 - 6 lbs.	sugar	2 - 3 kg
10 cups	hot water	2.5 L
3	lemons	3
6	oranges	6
2	bananas	2
2 lbs.	raisins	1 kg
2 tbsp.	dry yeast	30 mL

Combine the sugar and hot water in a saucepan. Heat until sugar is dissolved. Cool to lukewarm.

Chop the unpeeled lemons and oranges. Mash the bananas and finely chop the raisins. Add the fruit to the lukewarm sugar water. Sprinkle the yeast over the mixture. Keep it in a warm place and let it ferment for 1 month. Stir regularly during fermentation. Strain the mixture and bottle. Yields approximately 12 - 14 servings.

Champagne Gaspésien

4 à 6	livres de sucre	2-3 kg
5 pintes	d'eau chaude	2.5 L
3	citrons	3
6	oranges	6
2	bananas	2
2	livres de raisins	1 kg
2	paquets de levure sèche	30 mL

Dissoudre 4 à 6 livres de sucre dans 5 pintes d'eau chaude. Laissez tiédir et ajoutez 3 citrons et 6 oranges non pelés et tranchés, 2 bananes et 2 livres de raisins secs hachés finement.

Saupoudrez 2 paquets de levure sèche. Placez dans un endroit chaud et laissez fermenter durant un mois. Brassez souvent durant la fermentation. Coulez et embouteillez.

Forillon
National Park

Early Gaspé families made their own wine. Invited guests had the privilege of sampling the delights of the season. Local strawberries, black currants, rhubarb, and wheat were used to create these tantalizing wines!

Dandelion Wine

4 qts.	water	4L
4 qts.	dandelion blossoms	4 L
3 lbs.	sugar	1.5 kg
1	orange, peeled	1
1	lemon, peeled	1
⅛ tsp.	ginger root, grated	0.5 mL
1	slice bread	1
1 tbsp.	yeast	7 g
¼ cup	water	50 mL

Boil the 4 quarts of water. Pour into a large jar and when it is no longer steaming add dandelion blossoms. Cover with a cloth and set in a cool place. Stir often for 3 or 4 days. Strain.

Pour liquid into a large saucepan. Add sugar. Peel orange and lemon and set aside the peels. Chop the fruit and add to the sugar/water mixture. Add ginger root. Boil slowly for ½ hour. Remove from stove and allow to cool.

Toast bread and soak in a yeast/water solution. Add toast to cooled wine. Chop orange and lemon peel and add to the wine.

Leave wine in a warm place for 3 to 4 days. Strain, and bottle. Yields 5 - 5½ quarts (5 L).

Harold Beaumont
New Brunswick

Fundy National Park

Ginger Beer

3 gallons	boiling water	12 L
3 oz.	ginger	85 g
3 oz.	cream of tartar	85 g
3 lbs.	sugar	1.5 kg
3 tbsp.	yeast, put in when the mixture is cold	45 mL

Let it stand twenty-four hours and bottle. Good in three days.

This recipe is a typed copy of a original written in Isabel King's hand. It represents recipes which were typical of the middle class homes of the 1890's, where William Lyon Mackenzie King grew up. It is interesting to note the use of wine in cooking and the making of ginger beer in a temperance family. Yields 3 - 3½ gallons (12 L).

Kitchener, Ont.

Woodside
National Historic Park

Mount Revelstoke National Park

British Columbia

Mount Revelstoke National Park presents a contrast. The craggy peaks, gripped in perpetual ice and snow, stand in opposition to green carpeted valley floors.

These impressive heights lie in the Selkirk Range of the Columbia Mountains. This distinctive group is formed of ancient volcanic and metamorphic rock. For millions of years, water and ice have artistically carved the massive, steep, walled mountains with narrow valleys. These valleys are clothed with a luxurious rain forest of giant cedar and hemlock.

The seasons present a contrast as well. During the short summer months, the sub-alpine meadows are blanketed with a colour-burst of brilliant flower bouquets. In the winter, you can revel in a fairyland of soft snow-swirled trees. However, the winter can provoke the harshness of vicious snowslides thundering down steep mountainsides and the unpredictability of avalanches. This combination of dangerous avalanches, deep snows, narrow valleys, craggy peaks, and impenetrable forests has severely limited habitation of the Columbians. Throughout history, it has remained a wilderness refuge, undisturbed by man.

The interesting aspect of this park is that you don't need pitons, ropes, or hob-nailed boots to experience the exhilarating mountain view of this serene landscape. The Summit Road leads you to the peak of Mt. Revelstoke where you can leisurely enjoy the contrasts in this untouched wilderness.

Grey Owl's Recipe
for Home Brew

30-GALLON BATCH

3 gallons	molasses	12 L
40 lbs.	white sugar	20 kg
15 lbs.	beans	7.5 kg
6 pkg.	yeast cakes	6

10-GALLON BATCH

15 lbs.	potatoes, diced (boiled)	7.5 kg
15 lbs.	raisins (boiled first, retain juice)	7.5 kg
1 gallon	molasses	4 L
15 lbs.	dried apples	7.5 kg
5 lbs.	cornmeal	2.5 kg
3 pkg.	yeast cakes, as per bread dough, 1 hour dough risen	3

Grey Owl may have been terrific at making home brew, but he wasn't very good at writing down the instructions. We'll leave that to your imagination!

Grey Owl   *Prince Albert*
                                                    National Park

GREY OWL

Grey Owl, the colourful committed naturalist, author, and dynamic orator, lived for seven years in "Beaver Lodge" nestled snugly on the tree-lined shores of Ajawaan Lake, Prince Albert National Park. Here, he lovingly raised Rawhide and Jellyroll his precious beaver companions. Throughout his books, his love of the Canadian Wilderness and his concern for animal life touched the hearts of thousands.

To promote his beliefs, he consented to a tour of the British Isles in 1935. His appearance as a Canadian Indian deceived many but his stories of the Canadian wilderness rang true. He eagerly returned to Ajawaan Lake a tired man. This gentle peaceful conservationist contracted pneumonia and died on April 13, 1938.

Grey Owl had lived his dream! Out of the shadows, he came to speak his message and into the shadows he returned. Peacefully, he lies buried amid the spruce and aspen on the shores of Ajawaan Lake in his beloved wilderness. The lone grave site protectively overlooks the silent cabin and lake in the uninterrupted forests of Prince Albert National Park.

Shrimp Dip

8 oz.	cream cheese	250 g
1 cup	Miracle Whip salad dressing	250 mL
1 tsp.	dry mustard	5 mL
1 tsp.	Worcestershire sauce	5 mL
1 tsp.	tomato ketchup	5 mL
1 tsp.	lemon juice	5 mL
1 tbsp.	cream	15 mL
4	green onions, chopped	4
8 oz.	can broken shrimp, drained	250 g
¼ tsp.	salt	1 mL
⅛ tsp.	pepper	0.5 mL

Combine cream cheese, Miracle Whip, mustard, Worcestershire sauce, ketchup, lemon juice, and cream. Mix until smooth and creamy. Add onions, shrimp, salt, and pepper.

Place in a pretty bowl, sprinkle with paprika, and serve with crackers or potato chips. Yields 1½-2 cups of dip.

Sheila Gunn
Winnipeg, Man.

Riding Mountain
National Park

Crab-Stuffed Mushrooms

½ lb.	crabmeat	250 g
¼ cup	celery, chopped	50 mL
2 tbsp.	green pepper, chopped	30 mL
4	green onions, chopped	4
¼ cup	mayonnaise	50 mL
1 tsp.	Worcestershire sauce	5 mL
2-3 drops	Tabasco sauce	2-3 drops
1 tbsp.	chili sauce	15 mL
24	large fresh mushrooms	24
2 tbsp.	fine bread crumbs	30 mL
¼ cup	Swiss cheese, grated	50 mL
1 tbsp.	butter, melted	15 mL
½ tbsp.	parsley, chopped	7 mL

Preheat oven to 400°F (220°C). Flake the crabmeat. Combine crabmeat, celery, green pepper, onions, mayonnaise, Worcestershire sauce, Tabasco sauce, and chili sauce. Mix well.

Remove the stems from the washed mushrooms. Stuff the mushroom caps with the crab mixture.

Combine the crumbs, cheese, butter, and chopped parsley. Sprinkle over the stuffed mushrooms. Bake about 15 minutes or until golden brown. Before serving to guests, place hot mushrooms on a paper towel to absorb the juice. Serves 6.

Marilyn Cosgrove
Winnipeg, Man.

Riding Mountain
National Park

Glacier National Park

British Columbia

The ice-covered peaks, challenging glaciers, sheer mountain walls, and narrow valleys of Glacier National Park present a climax to the story of Canadian mountain scenery! The trails on the four hundred glaciers of this aptly named park are steep and treacherous. All forms of life in this park must survive within the limits of the landscape. It is a park for outdoor enthusiasts who accept the fierce challenge of pitting themselves against the natural elements. The rewards of the breath-taking views of majestic mountain peaks, avalanche-scarred valleys, and sparkling, jewel-encrusted glaciers provide a luring enticement!

Long winters, heavy snowfalls, and frequent avalanches create an annual "snow war" as man still struggles to cross the Selkirk Ranges through the Rogers Pass by rail or by highway.

For centuries, this area rested as a no-man's land. Indians and early explorers avoided the treacherous landscape. The dream of a cross-Canada railway instigated the search for a route through these steep ranges. After a massive struggle, against weather and land, the Canadian Pacific Railway managed to cross the Rogers Pass in 1886. Canada's first transcontinental railway became a reality!

This same struggle was relived when the Trans-Canada Highway forged its way through the Pass in 1962. The battle against incessant snows and an obstinate land continues every year as snowsheds are constantly maintained to protect avalanche vulnerable locations and artillery gunners trigger avalanches to stabilize threatening build-ups of snow.

The snow wars still persist in this rugged piece of landscape and many Canadians are accepting their challenge!

Lobster or Shrimp Balls

½ cup	lobster or shrimp (canned or fresh)	125 mL
4 oz.	cream cheese	125 g
1 tsp.	lemon juice	5 mL
¼ tsp.	Accent seasoning	1 mL
½ tsp.	salt	2 mL
1 tbsp.	celery, finely chopped	15 mL
⅛ tsp.	pepper	0.5 mL

Blend all ingredients together. Chill. Shape into balls about the size of cherries. Stick a pretzel stick into each ball, to serve as a handle. Refrigerate until serving. Makes about 15-20 balls.

Jean Smith
Nassau, Bahamas

Riding Mountain
National Park

Artichoke Fritatta

6	eggs	6
3 - 6 oz.	jars artichoke hearts, undrained marinated, sliced	3 - 170 mL
10	soda crackers, crushed	10
½ lb.	Cheddar cheese, grated	250 g

Beat eggs. Stir in artichoke hearts. Add crushed soda crackers and cheese.

Pour into a greased 9" x 13" (23 cm x 33 cm) pan. Bake 30 minutes at 350°F (180°C). Cut into squares. Makes about 18-20 hors d'oeuvres.

Note: This can be frozen after cooking.

Shirley Kirton
Scrases Meat Market, Wasagaming, Man.

Riding Mountain
National Park

The Scrases began their annual visits to the park in 1927 when they bought a cottage on the North Shore of Clear Lake. In 1939 they bought Scrases Meat Market and it has been a family-run business ever since.

Water Chestnut Rolls

3 tbsp.	soy sauce	45 mL
1½ tbsp.	sugar	22 mL
¼ cup	beef broth	50 mL
1 tbsp.	wine	15 mL
¼ tsp.	garlic salt	1 mL
6	whole water chestnuts, sliced	6
1	slice cooked ham	1
2	stalks green onion	2
12	strips lean bacon	12

Combine soy sauce, sugar, beef broth, wine, and garlic salt to make a marinade. Marinate water chestnut slices for 2-4 hours. (The longer you leave them, the more crunchy they become.)

Cut ham into 1" x 2" (2 cm x 5 cm) strips. Cut onion into ½" (1 cm) pieces.

Cut each bacon strip in half. Wrap 1 piece of bacon around a slice of water chestnut, a piece of onion, and a slice of ham. Secure with a toothpick.

Preheat oven to 375°F (190°C) and bake rolls approximately 15-18 minutes on the top rack.

Serve with a sweet and sour sauce as an appetizer or as a main dish. Yields 24 rolls.

Beth McKenzie
Calgary, Alta.

Riding Mountain
National Park

Mushroom Canapés

½ lb.	mushrooms, chopped	250 g
¼ cup	butter	1 mL
2 tbsp.	flour	30 mL
¾ tsp.	salt	4 mL
¼ tsp.	Accent seasoning	1 mL
1 cup	milk or cream	250 mL
2 tsp.	chives, minced	10 mL
	(or 1 tsp. (5 mL) onion salt)	
1 tsp.	lemon juice	5 mL
25	slices sandwich bread	25

Sauté mushrooms in butter for 5 minutes. Cool and then add flour, salt, and Accent. Stir in milk or cream and stir until thick. Add chives and lemon juice. Cool.

Remove crusts from bread. Flatten bread with a rolling pin. Place 1 tsp. (5 mL) of mushroom filling on each piece. Roll up each piece and cut into 3 pieces. Put them in the freezer.

To serve, brush each canapé with melted butter. Place on a cookie sheet and bake 15-20 minutes at 350°F (180°C). Makes about 75 appetizers.

Helen Hickling
Winnipeg, Man.

Riding Mountain
National Park

Blue Cheese Spread

1 lb.	blue cheese	500 g
½ lb.	soft butter	250 g
¾ lb.	soft cream cheese	365 g
2-3 tbsp.	brandy (to taste)	30-45 mL
	cayenne (to taste)	

Beat blue cheese. Add butter and cream cheese and beat well with Mixmaster. Flavour with a good shot of brandy or Scotch and a few grains of cayenne pepper. Beat again, taste and add another shot, etc.

I keep beating, adding Scotch and cayenne, until the buds are off and the tears start. (Add more Scotch than cayenne.) The flavour develops in the refrigerator. This keeps for several weeks in the refrigerator if well-covered. Makes about 3 cups of spread.

Les and Norma Gray
New Brunswick

Fundy
National Park

Crab Dip

8 oz.	cream cheese	250 g
2	green onions, chopped	2
2 tbsp.	Miracle Whip	30 mL
1 cup	crab meat	250 mL
	salt and pepper to taste	

Combine all ingredients, and mix well. Chill for at least 2 hours.

This is a delicious dip for either vegetables or chips. Makes 2-3 cups.

Carole Sheffield
Tofino, B.C.

Pacific Rim
National Park

Crab and Cheese Dip

1	medium onion, chopped	1
3	slices bacon, finely chopped	3
1	tomato, blanched	1
8 oz.	cream cheese	250 g
1 tbsp.	milk	15 mL
½ tsp.	horseradish	2 mL
¼ tsp.	salt	1 mL
⅛ tsp.	pepper	0.5 mL
6½ oz.	can crab meat	195 g
¼ tsp.	paprika	1 mL

Sauté onion and bacon in a little butter.

Chop tomato and add to onion/bacon mixture. Sauté for 2-3 minutes.

Combine all the ingredients except the paprika. Pour into a 1 quart (1 L) soufflé dish and sprinkle paprika on top.

Bake at 350°F (180°C) until hot and bubbly.

Let stand at room temperature 10 minutes before serving, to allow dip to set. Serve with crackers. Serves 4. (This dip can be frozen.)

Mary Porter
Dauphin, Man.

Riding Mountain
National Park

The Porters bought Mr. Henson's Drug Store at Clear Lake in the fall of 1949. This started their association with Riding Mountain National Park. Although the Porters still spend their summers at Clear Lake, the store was sold a few years later to the Meldrums, who still own it. It wouldn't seem like summer if you couldn't wander off the beach for an ice-cream cone at "Meldrums".

SOUPS, SALADS, & SIDE DISHES

Lobster Bisque, Dalvay-by-the-Sea

4 cups	milk	1 L
1	onion, sliced	1
¼ cup	butter	50 mL
2 tbsp.	flour	30 mL
1 lb.	lobster meat, cooked	500 g
½ cup	heavy or whipping cream	125 mL
3 tbsp.	tomato paste	45 mL
3 tbsp.	dry sherry	45 mL
1 tbsp.	pimiento, minced	15 mL
⅛ tsp.	cayenne	0.5 mL
¼ tsp.	salt (to taste)	1 mL
1 drop	Tabasco sauce (optional)	1 drop

In a saucepan, scald the milk with the sliced onion. Remove and discard the onion.

In another saucepan, melt the butter. Stir in the flour and cook over low heat, stirring constantly, for 3 minutes. Remove the pan from the heat. Add the scalded milk in a stream, whisking vigorously, and continue to whisk the mixture until it is smooth.

Pick over the lobster and cut into bite-sized pieces. Add the lobster, heavy cream, tomato paste, sherry, minced pimiento, and seasonings to the milk mixture. Cook over medium heat until it is just hot. Do not let it boil. Ladle the bisque into heated bowls. Serves 6.

Dalvay-by-the-Sea
Prince Edward Island

Prince Edward Island
National Park

Seafood Chowder

1 lb.	potatoes, peeled and cubed	500 g
8	slices bacon, diced	8
1 ½ cups	onion, chopped	375 mL
1 lb.	fish fillets	500 g
2 quarts	milk	2 L
½ lb.	scallops	250 g
2	Maggi chicken cubes	2
½ tsp.	pepper	2 mL
⅛ tsp.	thyme	0.5 mL
1 tsp.	salt (to taste)	5 mL

Cook potatoes in boiling salted water. Drain.

Fry bacon until crisp. Drain off fat, reserving ½ cup (125 mL). Remove bacon from frying pan and set aside. Sauté onions in the reserved bacon fat until tender.

Heat fish fillets in milk until almost boiling. Add potatoes, onions, bacon, and scallops. Simmer 5 minutes.

Dissolve the Maggi cubes in about 2 tbsp. (30 mL) of the milk from the chowder. Return this mixture to the chowder. Add the seasonings.
Serves 6 - 8.

Marina Collins
Alma, N.B.

Fundy
National Park

33

Recipe for Wagunabuie (Lichen) Soup

Pick moss and wash well.

Use the water in which fish, fish eggs, or meat has been boiled.

Remove any fish or meat and bring the water to a boil.

Add the moss.

Stir well while cooking.

Add salt for taste and boil until tender.

Now put the fish, fish eggs, or meat back into the water.

Stir and serve while hot.

This recipe was used during the era of Fort St. Joseph which was between 1796 and 1814. The Indians, at that time, used this recipe for Lichen Soup, which they called "Wagunabuie". The ingredients that they used are still available near the Fort even today!

During that era, the British and the Indians shared a strong friendly relationship. Without the help of these generous Indians, the garrison might have often gone hungry.

Ken McMillan
Richards Landing, Ont.

Fort St. Joseph
National Historic Park

Broccoli Chowder

2 lbs.	broccoli	1 kg
3 cups	chicken stock	750 mL
3 cups	milk	750 mL
1 cup	ham, chopped	250 mL
2 tsp.	salt	10 mL
⅛ tsp.	thyme	0.5 mL
⅛ tsp.	marjoram	0.5 mL
⅛ tsp.	pepper	0.5 mL
¼ cup	butter	50 mL
1 cup	half and half cream	250 mL
2 cups	Swiss cheese, grated	500 mL

Boil broccoli in 1½ cups chicken stock. Simmer 7 minutes or until fork tender. Remove broccoli from broth, chop coarsely and set aside. Add remaining chicken stock, milk, ham, salt, thyme, marjoram, and pepper. Stir well. Bring to a boil and cook over medium heat, stirring occasionally. Stir in butter, cream, cheese, and broccoli. Cook over medium heat until cheese is melted. Do not boil. Serves 8.

Mary Baxter
Winnipeg, Man.

Riding Mountain
National Park

Hamburger Soup

1½ lbs.	lean ground beef	750 g
1	medium onion, finely chopped	1
28 oz.	can tomatoes	796 mL
2 cups	water	500 mL
3 - 10 oz.	cans consommé	3 - 284 mL
10 oz.	can tomato soup	284 mL
4	carrots, finely chopped	4
1	bay leaf	1
3	celery stalks, finely chopped	3
1 tsp.	parsley flakes	5 mL
½ tsp.	thyme	2 mL
⅛ tsp.	pepper (to taste)	0.5 mL
½ cup	barley	125 mL

Brown meat and onions in a large frying pan. Drain well. Combine all ingredients in a large pot. Bring to a boil and simmer, covered, for about 2 hours. (This can also be cooked in a crock pot for 6-8 hours). Serves 8-10.

Serve with green salad and Irish bread. This is great when the gang arrives!

Bev Gowler
Winnipeg, Man.

Riding Mountain
National Park

Apple Onion Bisque

2 tbsp.	butter	30 mL
2 cups	onion, chopped	500 mL
2 cups	Golden Delicious apples, peeled, cored, and chopped	500 mL
1	clove garlic, crushed	1
½ tsp.	thyme, fresh or dried	2 mL
¼ tsp.	marjoram	1 mL
1	bay leaf	1
¼ tsp.	pepper, finely ground	1 mL
1 tsp.	coriander seeds, crushed	5 mL
4 cups	chicken stock (or 2 - 10 oz. (284 mL) cans chicken broth and equal amount of water)	1 L
¼ cup	whipping cream	50 mL
¼ tsp.	salt	1 mL
	fresh mint leaves, chopped (or dried mint leaves)	

Melt butter in a large saucepan. Sauté onion, apple, garlic, thyme, marjoram, bay leaf, pepper, and coriander for 10 minutes. Mixture should be fairly soft but not brown.

Add chicken broth. Bring to a boil. Reduce heat and simmer covered for 15 minutes.

Add cream and simmer for a few more minutes. Add salt to taste.

Pureé in blender or food processor until smooth. Serve hot or cold with fresh mint leaves sprinkled on top. Serves 4-6.

Betty Cuyler
Edmonton, Alta.

Jasper
National Park

Yoho National Park

British Columbia

This is the land of rock walls and waterfalls! The creeks and rivers tumble wildly down the western side of the continental divide, nurtured by moisture-laden Pacific air, icefields, and glaciers. One of the world's largest waterfalls, Takakkaw falls, flows magnificently into the Yoho Valley.

Because of the steep terrain and thick underbrush, native Indians established only temporary campsites in Yoho. Use of the area opened up only when Sir James Hector discovered the Kicking Horse Pass in 1858. It was christened with this name because he was kicked and nearly killed by his horse on the site. After much danger and excitement, the Canadian Pacific Railway completed their main line over the pass in 1885. Train wrecks and bottlenecks continually plagued the railway operation until the Spiral Tunnels opened in 1909.

With the overwhelming splendour of the waterfalls and the rocky summits, it is no wonder, that some very tiny, but fascinating, fossil formations lay hidden for centuries. Nestled in an area of transition, between the Eastern and Western main ranges of the Rockies, lie the fossils of the Burgess Shale. Charles Doolittle Walcott accidently discovered their silent resting place in 1901. His announcement, that he had discovered "some interesting things", was an understatement because the discovery proved so astounding that the Burgess Shale is now classified as a World Heritage Site.

The Shale takes us back 550 million years, to the Cambrian era when Yoho was covered by water. Mud slides from an adjacent reef carried living organisms into a basin on the sea floor. The absence of oxygen and predators left the site completely undisturbed. The silt gradually consolidated into shale, flattening the animal carcasses and leaving thin fossil impressions. Thus, 120 species were preserved to tell us of life in the beginnings of time. Some of these fossils represent creatures whose existence had never been suspected.

Amidst the glistening splendour of sparkling waterfalls, the peaceful tranquility of these fossils have recorded for us a major stage in the earth's evolutionary history and have shown us worlds beyond imagining.

Autumn Soup

1 lb.	ground beef	500 g
1 cup	onion, chopped	250 mL
4 cups	water	1 L
1 cup	carrots, chopped	250 mL
1 cup	celery, diced	250 mL
1 cup	potatoes, cubed, pared	250 mL
2 tsp.	salt	10 mL
1 tsp.	bottled brown bouquet sauce	5 mL
¼ tsp.	pepper	1 mL
1	bay leaf	1
⅛ tsp.	basil	0.5 mL
6	tomatoes*	6

In a large saucepan, cook and stir meat until brown. Drain off fat. Add onions. Cook and stir until onions are tender, about 5 minutes.

Stir in remaining ingredients, except the tomatoes. Bring to a boil. Reduce heat, cover and simmer 20 minutes.

Add tomatoes. Cover and simmer 10 minutes longer or until vegetables are tender.

*Note: A 28 oz. (796 mL) can tomatoes, with liquid can be substitued for the fresh tomatoes. Reduce water to 3 cups (750 mL). Stir in tomatoes with the rest of the ingredients and bring to a boil. Reduce heat, cover and simmer 20 minutes. The canned tomatoes break apart and give a rosy colour.

Serves 6.

Natalie Walker
Jasper, Alta.

Jasper
National Park

Mennonite Plumi Moos

2 quarts	boiling water	2 L
½ cup	raisins	125 mL
1 cup	dried mixed fruit	250 mL
¾ cup	sugar	175 mL
2 tbsp.	cornstarch	30 mL
1½ oz.	cherry Jell-o powder	42 g
½ tsp.	cinnamon	2 mL
½ tsp.	nutmeg	2 mL

Chop fruit in food processor. Cook fruit in boiling water until soft, 15-20 minutes.

Mix sugar and cornstarch with enough cold water to make a thin paste, about ½ cup (125 mL). Cook about 5 minutes, stirring constantly, until the starchy taste is gone. Remove from heat and add cherry Jell-o, cinnamon, and nutmeg.

Combine fruit mixture with Jell-o mixture and stir well. Cool. Soup will thicken as it cools. Served chilled.

Optional: Add 1 cup (250 mL) heavy cream or milk to the recipe to make it pink and creamy. (This is about 1 tbsp. (15 mL) per ½ cup (125 mL) serving.) Sprinkle cinnamon on top for a festive look! Serves 8-10.

Gail & Ralph Brown
Winnipeg, Man.

Prince Albert
National Park

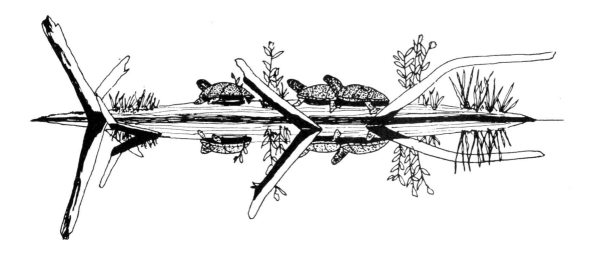

Chinese Cole Slaw

DRESSING:

½ cup	Kraft Calorie-Wise Cole Slaw Dressing	125 mL
½ tsp.	fresh ginger, grated (or ½ tsp. (2 mL) ground ginger)	2 mL

Combine salad dressing and ginger. Refrigerate in a covered jar for several hours or overnight, to let the flavours mingle.

SALAD:

4 cups	Chinese cabbage, shredded	1 L
1 cup	fresh parsley, chopped	250 mL
8 oz.	can pineapple tidbits, drained	250 mL
8 oz.	can water chestnuts, drained and sliced	250 mL

Combine Chinese cabbage, parsley, pineapple, and water chestnuts. Cover and chill until ready to serve. Just before serving, pour dressing over salad and toss to coat. Serves 10.

Rea Nesbitt
Winnipeg, Man.

Riding Mountain
National Park

See photograph page 96.

Cabbage Jellied Salad

3 oz.	package lime Jell-o	85 g
1 cup	boiling water	250 mL
2 tsp.	vinegar	10 mL
½ cup	cold water	125 mL
½ cup	mayonnaise	125 mL
½ cup	sour cream or yogurt	125 mL
2 tbsp.	pimiento, chopped	30 mL
1 tbsp.	prepared mustard	15 mL
1 tsp.	sugar	5 mL
2 tbsp.	onion, grated	30 mL
3 cups	cabbage, chopped	750 mL

Dissolve Jell-o in boiling water. Add vinegar and cold water. Chill until it begins to thicken. Add remaining ingredients, pour into a greased mold and chill. Serves 6.

Jean Lowes
Brandon, Man.

Riding Mountain
National Park

Sesame Spinach Salad

2 tbsp.	sesame seeds	30 mL
1/3 cup	vegetable oil	75 mL
1/4 cup	lemon juice	50 mL
2 tbsp.	soy sauce	30 mL
1 tsp.	salt	5 mL
1/8 tsp.	Tabasco sauce	0.5 mL
1/2 lb.	fresh mushrooms, thinly sliced	250 g
1 cup	water chestnuts, drained and sliced	250 mL
10 oz.	pkg. fresh spinach	300 g

Heat sesame seeds with oil in a large frying pan, until toasted and brown. Remove from heat. Combine lemon juice, soy sauce, salt, Tabasco sauce, and toasted sesame seeds. Mix well. Stir in mushrooms and water chestnuts. Cover and chill 3-4 hours.

Rinse spinach leaves. Drain well. Remove and discard tough stems and bruised leaves. Tear spinach into bite-sized pieces and place in a salad bowl. Just before serving, toss with mushroom dressing. Serves 8.

Gail & John Nesbitt
Stony Plain, Alta.

Banff & Riding Mountain
National Park

Beet Salad

14 oz.	can beets, drained and diced	398 mL
3/4 cup	beet juice	175 mL
3 oz.	pkg. orange Jell-o	85 g
1 cup	sour cream	250 mL
1 tbsp.	vinegar	15 mL

Drain beets, and reserve 3/4 cup (175 mL) juice. Bring beet juice to a boil. Add vinegar and dissolve Jell-o in the liquid. Cool slightly and add the sour cream. Beat with an egg beater until fluffy. Add the diced beets and pour into an oiled mold. Chill until firm. Serves 4-6.

Jean Smith
Nassau, Bahamas

Riding Mountain
National Park

Cherry Cranberry Salad

Layer 1:

20 oz.	can red tart sour cherries, pitted	600 mL
1 cup	cherry juice	250 mL
3 oz.	pkg. cherry Jell-o	85 g
1 cup	jellied cranberry sauce	250 mL

Drain cherries. Reserve the juice and add enough water to make 1 cup. Bring juice to a boil. Add Jell-o and stir until dissolved. Add drained cherries. Pour into a 9" x 9" x 2" (23 cm x 23 cm x 5 cm) baking dish and chill until almost firm.

Layer 2:

3 oz.	pkg. lemon Jell-o	85g
1 cup	boiling water	250 mL
3 oz.	cream cheese	85 g
⅓ cup	mayonnaise	75 mL
1 cup	crushed pineapple (including liquid)	250 mL
2 oz.	envelope Dream Whip	60 g
1 cup	mini marshmallows	250 mL
2 tbsp.	nuts, chopped	30 mL

Dissolve Jell-o in boiling water. Soften cream cheese with the mayonnaise and gradually add to the lemon Jell-o. Stir in the undrained crushed pineapple. Chill until partially set.

Whip Dream Whip according to package directions. Fold into partially set lemon Jell-o mixture. Add mini marshmallows. Spread over the chilled cranberry cherry layer. Sprinkle with nuts. Cover and chill until firm. Serves 8-10.

Betty Ansley
Kimberley, B.C.

Riding Mountain
National Park

See photograph page 96.

Kootenay National Park

British Columbia

Legend has it that Woodpecker and the animal people were plagued by the monstrous "Deep Water Dweller". During this crisis, they found the "Old Grandfather of the Kootenais" crawling over the countryside, stopping at each place to give it a name. They implored this "Tall Person" to drive the monster out of the water. Old Grandfather waded into the sky blue waters, kicked at the Deep Water Dweller, but missed. The beast fled into the very source of the stream under the mountains. The man broke off a piece of a mountain, solidified it with his knees, and built a dam to trap the monster. When Woodpecker killed the serpent, the blood, which was really water, flowed from the monster's wounds. It flooded the area and forced the Kootenai people to flee to the mountains. The Deep Water Dweller was cut up and thrown down the Kootenay river where the remnants formed the cliffs and other features of the landscape. This was the dramatic beginning of a land with deep spiritual significance and artistic attraction!

The Kootenai Indians also had a special reverence for the Paint Pots in Kootenay National Park. Here, an active cold spring bubbles to the surface. The iron dissolved in it forms muddy beds of reddish ochre. The Kootenais would travel for days to obtain the prized ochre and vermilion pigments that were used to paint their bodies and teepees.

Radium Hot Springs was the sacred territory of Nipika, a powerful guardian spirit. These springs provided a treasured meeting place for Indian tribes as they travelled north and south on their river routes. This tradition continues today, as people gather to enjoy the warm, soothing pleasures of these Hot Springs. The springs begin with water that drains down interconnected faults from rainfall run-off. The earth's core temperatures transform these trickling waters into delicate vapours. As the vapour seeks its way cautiously to the surface it reverts to the bubbling, luminous springs that have attracted people for centuries.

Kootenay National Park has long been a unique place of imagination and inspiration. It is a land created in legend and preserved in reality.

Mustard Gelatin Ring

4	eggs	4
¾ cup	sugar	175 mL
1 tbsp.	unflavoured gelatin	7 g
1½ tbsp.	dry mustard	22 mL
½ tsp.	turmeric	2 mL
¼ tsp.	salt	1 mL
1 cup	water	250 mL
½ cup	cider vinegar	125 mL
½ cup	whipping cream	125 mL
	cole slaw, mixed with pineapple chunks, chicory, watercress, or other greens	

Beat eggs, and set aside. Mix together sugar and unflavoured gelatin. Stir in mustard, turmeric, and salt.

Add water and vinegar to the beaten eggs. Stir in sugar gelatin mixture and cook in double boiler over boiling water until slightly thickened, stirring constantly. Cool until mixture is thick.

Whip cream and stir in. Pour mixture into a 1½ quart (1.5 L) ring mold. Chill until firm. Unmold and, if desired, fill center with cole slaw pineapple mixture. Garnish with chilled greens. Delicious with baked ham, particularly in the summer. Serves 6-8.

Dorothy Cosgrove
Winnipeg, Man.

Riding Mountain
National Park

Five generations of the Cosgroves have enjoyed summer pleasure at their cottage in Riding Mountain National Park since they first leased the property in 1932.

Chicken or Tuna Jellied Salad

1 tbsp.	Knox unflavoured gelatin	7 g
½ cup	cold water	125 mL
10 oz.	can cream of chicken or cream of mushroom soup	284 mL
½ cup	cold water	125 mL
1 tbsp.	lemon juice	15 mL
⅛ tsp.	pepper	0.5 mL
1 cup	chicken, turkey, or tuna boned, diced	250 mL
½ cup	celery, chopped	125 mL
¼ cup	green pepper, chopped	50 mL
2 tbsp.	pimiento, chopped	30 mL
2 tsp.	onion, grated	10 mL

In the top of a double boiler, sprinkle gelatin over ½ cup (125 mL) cold water. Place over boiling water and stir until dissolved.

Blend soup with ½ cup (125 mL) cold water. Add gelatin, lemon juice, and pepper. Mix well and chill until the mixture starts to set.

Fold in chicken, turkey, or tuna, green pepper, pimiento, and onion. Turn into an oiled mold. Chill until firm. Serves 4-6.

May Hawking
Wasagaming, Man.

Riding Mountain
National Park

Quick Tomato Aspic

1 tbsp.	Knox unflavoured gelatin	7 g
½ tsp.	celery salt	2 mL
½ tsp.	onion salt	2 mL
⅛ tsp.	pepper	0.5 mL
2 cups	tomato juice	500 mL
½ cup	diced celery, green onion, green pepper, or a combination of all 3 (optional)	125 mL

Combine first 5 ingredients in a saucepan. Place over medium heat, and stir constantly until gelatin dissolves (about 3-5 minutes).

Pour into mold. Chill. When aspic is slightly thickened, add celery, onion, and green pepper if desired. Serves 4.

May Hawking
Wasagaming, Man.

Riding Mountain
National Park

Marinated Mushrooms

¼ cup	vegetable oil	50 mL
3 tbsp.	wine vinegar	45 mL
⅓ cup	tomato juice	75 mL
1 tsp.	salt	5 mL
1 tsp.	paprika	5 mL
½ tsp.	black pepper	2 mL
2	cloves garlic	2
2 lbs.	small mushrooms	1 kg

Combine all ingredients, except the mushrooms, in a screw top jar and chill for several days. Remove the garlic.

Add the mushrooms and marinate for several days. Shake or stir occasionally. These mushrooms may be used as an appetizer, added to salads, or used as a garnish. Use the marinade as a salad dressing for a green salad.

Doris Hatt
Alma, N.B.

Fundy
National Park

Sour Milk Salad Dressing

⅔ cup	sugar	150 mL
1 tsp.	salt	5 mL
1 tbsp.	dry mustard	15 mL
1 tbsp.	cornstarch	15 mL
½ cup	vinegar	125 mL
2 tbsp.	water	30 mL
1 cup	sour milk	250 mL
1	egg, beaten	1
1 tbsp.	margarine	15 mL

Combine sugar, salt, mustard, and cornstarch in a double boiler. Gradually add vinegar, water, sour milk, and beaten egg, stirring until smooth. Cook until thickened. Remove from heat and add margarine.

This dressing is especially good in sandwich fillings. Makes about 2 cups of dressing.

Melva E. Crawford
Ladner, B.C.

Riding Mountain
National Park

Melva is 94 years old, and has enjoyed summers at Clear Lake since 1931.

Thousand Island Dressing

1 cup	mayonnaise	250 mL
1 tbsp.	onion, finely chopped	15 mL
1	small, firm, red tomato, finely chopped or puréed	1
¼ tsp.	mustard	1 mL
1 tbsp.	red pepper, chopped	15 mL
1 tbsp.	green pepper, chopped	15 mL
1 tbsp.	celery, chopped	15 mL
4-6	olives, chopped	4-6
1	hard-boiled egg, chopped	1
¼ tsp.	Tabasco sauce	1 mL
¼ tsp.	paprika	1 mL
¼ tsp.	French tarragon, very finely chopped	1 mL

Mix all the ingredients together and chill.

No recipe book should be without this famous dressing, developed just across the border from St. Lawrence Islands National Park, on the U.S. side of the St. Lawrence. It was produced for George Boldt, owner of the Waldorf Astoria by his famous chef "Oscar". There are many versions and the original is still a secret. However, this is close! Makes 1½-2 cups of dressing.

Keith Dewar
Smiths Falls, Ont.

St. Lawrence Islands
National Park

Summer Slaw Dressing — Elk Horn Ranch

½ cup	sugar	125 mL
½ tsp.	salt	2 mL
½ tsp.	dry mustard	2 mL
½ tsp.	flour	2 mL
1	egg	1
¾ cup	oil	175 mL
½ cup	vinegar	125 mL

Using a blender or eggbeater, mix together sugar, salt, mustard, flour, and egg.

Slowly add oil, beating well between additions. Then add vinegar, beating well. Store in the refrigerator. Shake before using. This refrigerator dressing is excellent on greens as well as on cole slaw. Makes about 2 cups of dressing.

Ruth Aikens
Wasagaming, Man.

Riding Mountain
National Park

This recipe was served as the house dressing at the Elk Horn Ranch. Lorne and Ruth Aikens owned the Elk Horn Ranch for 10 years and it became noted for its congenial hospitality and good food, as well as for varied recreational pursuits.

Zucchini Casserole

6 cups	zucchini, diced	1.5 L
1 cup	carrots, grated	250 mL
¼ cup	onion, finely chopped	50 mL
4 cups	cheese croutons	1 L
½ cup	margarine	125 mL
1½ cups	evaporated milk	375 mL
10 oz.	can mushroom soup	284 mL
⅛ tsp.	poultry seasoning	0.5 mL

Simmer zucchini, carrots and onions 5 minutes in salted water. Sauté croutons in margarine. Place ⅔ of the croutons in a greased 2 quart (2 L) casserole. Mix vegetables with milk, soup, and seasoning. Pour over croutons. Top with remaining croutons. Bake 30 minutes at 350°F (180°C). Serves 6-8.

Ethel Lisowski
Brandon, Man.

Riding Mountain
National Park

Turnips and Apples

2	large turnips	2
2 tbsp.	butter	30 mL
4	apples	4
½ cup	brown sugar	125 mL
¼ tsp.	cinnamon	1 mL
⅓ cup	flour	75 mL
⅓ cup	brown sugar	75 mL
2 tbsp.	butter	30 mL

Peel, dice, and cook turnips until tender. Add butter, and mash.

Peel and slice the apples. Toss the apples with ½ cup (125 mL) brown sugar and cinnamon. Arrange the apples and turnips in a buttered 1 quart (1 L) casserole in alternate layers - beginning and ending with the turnips.

Combine the flour, ⅓ cup (75 mL) brown sugar and butter until crumbly. Sprinkle on top of the casserole.

Bake for 1 hour at 350°F (180°C). Microwave — Cook at level "6" for approximately 35-40 minutes. Serves 4-6.

Sally Shwetz
Winnipeg, Man.

Riding Mountain
National Park

Sally is associated with Camp Wasaga in Riding Mountain National Park. Through the activities of this camp, United Church campers have been discovering the wonders of nature and the recreational activities of this versatile park since 1925. The first camps concentrated on youth programs sponsored by local presbyteries. However, in the last decade, Camp Wasaga has developed an innovative family camping program which encourages interaction with the natural surroundings and fosters family memories as well!

Corn Husking

In the late 1800's Corn Husking parties were an annual event. Towards the beginning of autumn, each family called together their neighbours and friends to husk corn. This task then became a party. Music was played, tricks were played, stories were told, and, of course, every young man kept a sharp eye out for the famous and rare "red ear" which would permit him to kiss his favourite young lady!

Villes-des-Laurentides, Qué.   *Sir Wilfrid Laurier House*
National Historic Park

Au début de L'automne, chaque famille réunissait voisins et amis pour éplucher la provision de blé d'inde". Cette corvée, mieux connue sous le nom "épluchette de blé d'inde", donnait lieu á de nombreuses réjouissances: on jouait de la musique, on se jouait des tours, on se racontait des histoires et on guettait bien sûr, le fameux (épi rouge) qui devait permettre á l'un des jeunes hommes d'embrasser sa belle! . . .

Ville-des-Laurentides, Qué.   *La Maison de Sir Wilfrid Laurier*
Parc Historique National

Waterton Lakes National Park

Alberta

This park is a meeting place, an area of sharing. The prairie rolls up to meet the flanks of snow-capped mountains and alpine lakes nestled in lush alpine meadows. The community of Waterton Park is, perched on the fan of a stream flowing into Upper Waterton Lake, the deepest lake in the Rockies.

It is a merging of past and present, with a billion years of geological history written on the richly coloured mountains. Some of the oldest bedrock in the Rockies is exposed here. Glaciation played its part in carving out lakes and resculpturing valleys, leaving hanging valleys and waterfalls and depositing a rolling landscape of glacial moraines, eskers, and kames.

Waterton's first permanent resident, John George "Kootenai" Brown, a small agile man with a quick eye, became the park's first superintendent. Kootenai served in the British Army in India in the 1850's before heading to the Cariboo gold rush. He later became a scout for the United States Army, a "Pony Express" mail rider, a Rocky Mountain Ranger, a hunter, and a trader. This colourful character was acquitted of killing another trader before settling in what was to become Waterton Lakes National Park in 1878.

Kootenai served the rest of his life with the National Park Service in Waterton, with interruptions to become a guide and packer for the North West Mounted Police. He died in the park in 1916 and is buried peacefully on the shores of Lower Waterton Lake.

Archaeological sites indicate that there were other residents in this area during pre-historic times. The region was also shared, at different seasons of the year, by the powerful Blackfoot Nation of the Great Plains and the Kootenai tribes of the mountains of Alberta and British Columbia.

The area is still shared with Glacier National Park in Montana. In 1932, the two became the world's first International Peace Park. The two parks share a number of lakes and are linked by tour boats, trails, and an international highway. In the International Peace Park, you can stand in two countries at the same time while catching a fish of dual citizenship.

The two parks, local ranchers, industry, and provincial agencies have been working together to integrate conservation and use of the region's natural resources. They may become the world's first International Biosphere Reserve. This will truly preserve the area as a symbol of sharing and peace!

Marinated Carrots

2 lbs.	carrots, cut in strips	1 kg
10 oz.	can tomato soup	284 mL
½ cup	vegetable oil	125 mL
¼ cup	sugar	50 mL
¼ cup	vinegar	50 mL
1 tsp.	dry mustard	5 mL
1 tsp.	Worcestershire sauce	5 mL
½ tsp.	salt	2 mL
⅛ tsp.	pepper	0.5 mL
1	green pepper, chopped	1
1	onion, chopped or sliced	1

Cook carrots in a little salted water until slightly crunchy. Drain.

Mix soup, oil, sugar, vinegar, and seasonings in food processor or blender. Bring to a boil, and pour over drained carrots, green pepper, and onion. Marinate overnight.

This keeps well refrigerated and is delicious served hot or cold. Serves 6-8.

Pamela McKay
Ingonish Beach, N.S.

Cape Breton Highlands
National Park

Vegetable and Bacon Quiche

6 slices	bacon	6
1	onion, chopped	1
4 cups	broccoli and cauliflower pieces, cooked	1 L
6	eggs, beaten	6
2 cups	medium or sharp Cheddar cheese, grated	500 mL
½ tsp.	salt	2 mL
½ tsp.	marjoram	2 mL
½ tsp.	sweet basil	2 mL
1	unbaked 9" (23 cm) pie shell	1

Fry bacon until crisp. Pour off ½ of the drippings. Add onion and vegetables. Sauté lightly. Cover and braise for 2 minutes.

Remove from heat and stir in eggs, cheese, salt, and herbs. Combine well. Pour into pie shell and bake 30-40 minutes at 325°F (160°C) or until set. Makes 6-8 servings.

Marj Stewart
Winnipeg, Man.

Riding Mountain
National Park

Zucchini Quiche

	pastry for 9" (23 cm) pie	
2 tsp.	Dijon or prepared mustard (optional)	10 mL
½ cup	butter	125 mL
4 cups	zucchini, sliced	1 L
1 cup	onion, coarsely chopped	250 mL
½ cup	fresh parsley, chopped	125 mL
	OR	
2 tbsp.	dried parsley	30 mL
½ tsp.	salt	2 mL
½ tsp.	black pepper	2 mL
¼ tsp.	garlic powder	1 mL
½ tsp.	basil	2 mL
¼ tsp.	oregano	1 mL
2	eggs, well-beaten	2
2 cups	shredded Muenster, mozzarella or other cheese	500 mL

Use your favourite recipe for the pie crust. Prick it with many holes, and precook 10 minutes at 450°F (230°C). (It may shrink a little.) If it starts to puff up, prick more holes. Remove from oven and spread prepared mustard over the bottom.

In a large skillet, melt butter. Stir-fry zucchini, onion, and seasonings, about 10 minutes.

In a large bowl, beat the eggs. Add shredded cheese and zucchini mixture. Mix well and spread in precooked pie shell.

Bake 30 minutes at 350°F (180 C). Let cool a few minutes before cutting. Serves 4-6. (This goes nicely with a fresh green salad.)

Margot and Barry Spencer
Richibucto, N.B.

Kouchibouguac
National Park

Lefse

7 cups	mashed potatoes	1.75 L
½ cup	cream	125 mL
1½ cups	flour	375 mL
2½ cups	flour	625 mL

Combine mashed potatoes and cream. Set aside to cool.

Add 1½ cups (375 mL) flour to cooled potatoes and mix well. Form dough into balls the size of an egg. Roll out the balls in the remaining flour. Make thin, ⅛″ (3 mm) circles.

Fry on a hot, lightly greased griddle. Turn over when the bottom side is brown in spots. (If they become hard, the heat is too low.)

As the cakes are done, place them on a tea towel. Stack 12-16 cakes on each towel. Wrap them up in the towel, and store them in a cool place.

Lefse may be rolled up as crêpes, or served as flat cakes, to be buttered like bread or sprinkled with brown sugar and cinnamon. Yields approximately 4-6 dozen.

This recipe is symbolic of the Scandinavian way of life. I am proud to carry on the custom which originated in the Scandinavian countries. We always have Lefse served with lutefisk on Christmas Eve.

Janice Furevick
Erickson, Man.

Riding Mountain
National Park

Pyrohy

2 tbsp.	butter, melted	30 mL
¾ cup	milk	175 mL
1	egg, well-beaten	1
2½ cups	flour	625 mL
½ tsp.	salt	2 mL
12	potatoes, mashed (hot)	12
½ lb.	Cheddar cheese, grated	250 g
½ lb.	cream cheese	250 g

Mix melted butter, milk, and egg. Sift flour and salt. Add liquid to flour and mix well. Knead until dough is smooth and elastic. Cover and leave in a warm place for 2 hours.

Combine potatoes, Cheddar cheese and cream cheese.

Roll dough out thinly. Cut into 2" (5 cm) circles. Place a teaspoon of potato filling on each circle. Fold over and pinch the edges together to seal.

Drop pyrohy into salted boiling water. Boil 8-10 minutes. Drain. Dot with butter and serve hot with sour cream.

Mrs. Wawrykow,
Brandon, Man.

Riding Mountain
National Park

Buffet Potatoes

2 lbs.	frozen hash brown potatoes	1 kg
2 cups	sour cream	500 mL
2 - 10 oz.	cans cream of mushroom soup	2 - 284 mL
½ cup	margarine, melted	125 mL
2 cups	Cheddar cheese, grated	500 mL
½ cup	onion, chopped (optional)	125 mL
	Parmesan cheese	

Mix all ingredients together except Parmesan cheese. Spread in a greased 9" x 13" x 2" (23 cm x 33 cm x 5 cm) pan. Sprinkle Parmesan cheese on top. Bake 1 hour at 350°F (180°C). Serves 10.

Betty Rose
Summerland, B.C.

Riding Mountain
National Park

Lac du Bonnet Rice

⅔-1 cup	wild rice	150-250 mL
3 cups	boiling water	750 mL
½ tsp.	salt	2mL
½ lb.	bacon	250 g
½ cup	celery, chopped	125 mL
1	onion, chopped	1
10 oz.	can chicken broth	284 mL
10 oz.	can water	284 mL
10 oz.	can mushrooms	284 mL
	OR	
1 cup	fresh mushrooms	250 mL
½ cup	slivered almonds	125 mL
1 tbsp.	butter	15 mL

Put rice into a strainer and wash with cold running water.

Stir rice into boiling water and salt. Parboil for 5 minutes. Remove from heat and let the rice soak in the same water, covered, for 1 hour. Drain and wash again.

Fry bacon, celery, and onion until bacon is crisp and celery and onion are tender. Drain off excess fat.

Grease a 2 quart (2 L) casserole and combine chicken broth, water, rice, bacon, celery, onion, mushrooms, and almonds.

Bake, covered, for 1-1½ hours at 350°F (180°C). Check the rice midway through the cooking period to see if it is dry. If so, add a little more water.

Before serving, dot with butter. Serves 8.

John and Gail Nesbitt
Stony Plain, Alta.

Banff and Riding Mountain
National Park

Wild Rice Casserole

1 cup	wild rice [or ½ cup (125 mL) brown rice,	250 mL
3 cups	boiling water	750 mL
½ cup	(125 mL) wild rice]	
½ cup	butter	125 mL
1	green pepper, chopped	1
8	celery stalks, chopped	8
1	large Spanish onion, chopped	1
10 oz.	can button mushrooms and liquid	284 mL
10 oz.	can consommé soup	284 mL
1 tsp.	poultry seasoning	5 mL
1	bay leaf	1
½ tsp.	salt	2 mL
¼ tsp.	pepper	1 mL

Wash rice under cold water. Drain. Pour boiling water over rice. Soak overnight. Boil rice, in soaking water, 30 minutes. Drain off liquid and set aside.

Sauté butter, green pepper, celery, and onion in a large frying pan. Add remaining ingredients, including rice. Cook for 3 minutes on top of stove. Pour into a 2 quart (2 L) casserole. Cover tightly. Bake 1 hour at 350°F (180°C). Makes 8 generous servings. (This can be frozen.)

Donna Johnson
Winnipeg, Man.

Riding Mountain
National Park

Green Rice

3 cups	cooked rice	750 mL
½ cup	green olives, chopped	125 mL
1 cup	mushrooms	250 mL
1 cup	onion, chopped	250 mL
1 cup	celery, chopped	250 mL
¼ cup	parsley, chopped	50 mL
½ cup	green pepper, chopped	125 mL
10 oz.	can Cheddar cheese soup	284 mL
½ cup	cheese, grated	125 mL
½ cup	bread crumbs	125 mL

Combine all ingredients except grated cheese and bread crumbs. Pour into a greased 2 quart (2 L) casserole. Top with grated cheese and crumbs. Bake for 30 minutes at 325°F (160°C). Serves 4-6.

Marj Stewart
Winnipeg, Man.

Riding Mountain
National Park

See photograph page 96.

Eggs Goldenrod

Chateau Lake Louise

6	hard-cooked eggs	6
2 cups	medium white sauce (recipe to follow)	500 mL
1 tbsp.	parsley, chopped	15 mL
6	slices hot toast, buttered	6
1/4 tsp.	paprika	1 mL

Cut the eggs in half and remove the yolks. Cut egg whites in lengthwise slices.

Heat the white sauce and add the egg whites and parsley.

Meanwhile, pass the yolks through a sieve. Prepare the toast. Pour some egg sauce over each slice. Sprinkle with sieved egg yolk and paprika. Serves 6.

WHITE SAUCE

4 tbsp.	butter	60 mL
4 tbsp.	flour	60 mL
2 cups	milk	500 mL
1/2 tsp.	salt	2 mL
1/4 tsp.	white pepper	1 mL
1/4 tsp.	dry mustard	1 mL

Melt the butter in the top of a double boiler. Stir in the flour and mix until smooth. Gradually add milk, stirring constantly. Simmer and stir until the sauce has thickened.

Jaroslav Nydr, Executive Chef   *Banff*
Chateau Lake Louise   *National Park*

See photograph page 16.

MEAT

&

DINNER DISHES

Beef Strips in Red Wine and Basil

2 - 6-8 oz.	sirloin steaks	2 - 180-250 g
2 tbsp.	butter	30 mL
1	small onion, chopped	1
1 tsp.	tomato paste	5 mL
1 tbsp.	flour	15 mL
½ cup	beef stock, bouillon, or broth	125 mL
½ cup	dry red wine	125 mL
	juice of ½ small lemon	
¼-½ tsp.	basil	1-2 ml.
	parsley for garnish	
¼ tsp.	salt	1 mL
⅛ tsp.	pepper	0.5 mL

Cut steak into strips. Sauté in foaming butter over high heat. Add onions, cook with beef until onions are softened. Stir the beef strips constantly to prevent them from burning.

Lower heat. Add tomato paste and flour and cook for a minute. Stir until flour has absorbed the butter and pan juices.

Add beef stock and wine, stir to form a smooth sauce. Add lemon juice, basil, salt, and pepper. Continue to cook for 5 minutes or until beef is tender. Garnish with parsley and serve on a bed of rice. Serves 2.

Jeanne (Gregersen) Christensen
Prior Lake, Minn., USA

Riding Mountain
National Park

Barbecue Oven Steak

1½ lbs.	steak, cut into serving-size pieces	750 g
3 tbsp.	margarine	45 mL
½ cup	onion, chopped	125 mL
½ cup	celery, chopped	125 mL
1 tbsp.	vinegar	15 mL
10 oz.	can tomato soup	284 mL
3 tbsp.	brown sugar	45 mL
2 tbsp.	Worcestershire sauce	30 mL
⅛ tsp.	salt	0.5 mL
⅛ tsp.	pepper	0.5 mL
1	clove garlic	1

Brown meat in margarine. Place in a shallow 2 quart (2 L) baking dish. Combine remaining ingredients. Pour over steak. Cover pan and bake for 1½-2 hours at 350°F (180°C). Serves 4-5.

Beverley Rutherford
Field, B.C.

Yoho
National Park

Banff National Park

Alberta

Canada's first National Park is renowned as a resort area. Millions of visitors are lured to this park each year to enjoy the splendour and magnificence of the rugged snow-capped peaks and enticing meadow-green valleys.

The origins of the present day resort date back to 1883. Two railway construction workers, turned prospectors, came up the slopes by hand car on the newly laid railway line and crossed the swift Bow River on a rough raft. They accidently discovered the Cave and Basin Hot Springs which have warm sulphurous waters. The springs became so popular that they attracted the attention of men such as William Van Horne, president of the Canadian Pacific Railway. Realizing the potential of the area, the railway built the Banff Springs Hotel and, later, the Chateau Lake Louise which enticed the rich and powerful from all over the world. The railway company encouraged alpine activity by importing Swiss guides and hiring local guides. The most famous of these guides, were of course, the Brewsters who became the official guides and outfitters to the Banff Springs Hotel. This venture grew into the largest transportation company in the Canadian Rockies. The Brewsters had a share in opening up the area and allowing people from all over the world to savour the silence and peace of this Canadian wilderness.

The spirit of the Brewsters is enshrined on the challenging peak of Mt. Brewster, a skier's paradise of majestic soft silky snows and mountains!

Fortunately, for us, the railway was not the only group that saw the potential of the area. And in 1885, a far-sighted government set aside a portion of Sulphur Mountain for future park use. This has since been expanded to preserve the entire area for future generations to enjoy as much as we do.

Although many think of Banff in terms of only being a modern-day resort, it has been a popular haven for centuries. Plentiful food and a favourable climate attracted prehistoric man to the area and, later, the Kootenai, Assiniboine, and Cree Indians enjoyed the bounty of this land.

To consider Banff National Park as just a resort is a tremendous injustice. It is the inherent grandeur and richness of the wilderness that draws people to the area. The encompassing solitude of a wilderness hike is refreshing and renewing. Few forget the exhilaration of kayaking or canoeing on the mighty Bow River. It is these experiences, preserved and nurtured, that will continue to dangle as a tantalizing lure to future generations.

Veal Ragout

1 lb.	veal	500 g
2 tbsp.	parsley	30 mL
2	bay leaves	2
¼ tsp.	thyme	1 mL
1½ tsp.	salt	7 mL
3 cups	water	750 mL
1	onion, chopped	1
2	carrots, quartered	2
2	stalks celery, quartered	2
10 oz.	can mushrooms	284 mL
¼ cup	butter	50 mL
¼ cup	flour	50 mL
1 tsp.	salt	5 mL
1 cup	light cream	250 mL

Cut veal into bite-sized pieces. Combine veal, parlsey, bay leaves, thyme, salt, and water in a 2 quart (2 L) saucepan. Cover. Bring to a boil. Reduce heat and simmer for 30 minutes.

Add vegetables and cook another 30 minutes.

Remove from heat, and pour off the broth. Drain the mushrooms, reserving the juice. Add enough water and mushroom juice to the broth to make 4 cups (1 L).

Melt butter. Add flour, stirring until smooth. Add salt, cream, and broth. Cook until mixture thickens. Add mushrooms.

Pour sauce over veal and vegetables. Stir and cook over low heat until thoroughly heated.

Serve over rice. Serves 4-6.

Linda Dinsdale
Vancouver, B.C.

Riding Mountain
National Park

French Bread, Ham and Cheese Fondue

3 cups	French bread, cubed	750 mL
3 cups	cooked ham, cubed	750 mL
½ lb.	Cheddar cheese, cubed 1" (2.5 cm) cubes	250 g
3 tbsp.	flour	45 mL
1 tbsp.	dry mustard	15 mL
3 tbsp.	butter, melted	45 mL
4	eggs	4
3 cups	milk	750 mL
¼ tsp.	Worcestershire sauce	0.5 mL

Layer ⅓ of the bread cubes, ⅓ of the ham and ⅓ of the cheese in a 2 quart (2 L) casserole.

Combine flour and mustard and sprinkle 1 tbsp. (15 mL) over the first 3 layers. Drizzle 1 tbsp. melted butter on top. Repeat this procedure for 2 more layers.

Beat egg, milk, and Worcestershire sauce. Pour over casserole. Chill 4 hours or overnight. Bake, covered, 1 hour at 350°F (180°C) or until puffed and golden. Serves 6.

Thelma Bolduc
Ottawa, Ont.

Riding Mountain
National Park

Crescent Sausage and Cheese Bake

8 oz.	can Pillsbury Crescent Rolls	250 g
8 oz.	pkg. sausages, cooked	250 g
2 cups	Swiss or Monterey cheese, shredded	500 mL
4	eggs, slightly beaten	4
¾ cup	milk	175 mL
2 tbsp.	green pepper, chopped	30 mL
¼ tsp.	oregano	1 mL
¼ tsp.	salt	1 mL
¼ tsp.	pepper	1 mL

Separate dough into 2 rectangles. Press into a 10"x8" (25 cm x 20 cm) pan, covering the bottom and ½" (1.3 cm) up the sides. Seal perforations.

Slice sausages about ½" (1.3 cm) thick and place over crust. Sprinkle cheese on top. Combine remaining ingredients, pour over cheese and sausages.

Bake 20-25 minutes at 400-425°F (220°C) until crust is golden brown. Serve with salad. Serves 4-6.

Shirley Willoughby
London, Ont.

Riding Mountain
National Park

Sweet and Sour Meatballs

SAUCE

1	green pepper, chopped	1
1	onion, chopped	1
2	celery stalks, chopped	2
2 tbsp.	oil	30 mL
2 - 10 oz.	cans tomato soup	2 - 284 mL
1 cup	lukewarm water	250 mL
3 tbsp.	brown sugar	45 mL
2 tbsp.	vinegar	30 mL
3 drops	Worcestershire sauce	3 drops
3 tbsp.	hamburger relish	45 mL

Sauté green pepper, onion, and celery in hot oil.

Add tomato soup and water. Stir in brown sugar, vinegar, Worcestershire sauce, and relish. Simmer for about 10 minutes. While sauce is cooking, prepare meatballs.

MEATBALLS

1 lb.	ground beef	500 g
2 tbsp.	hamburger relish	15 mL
¼ cup	bread crumbs	50 mL
1	egg	1
¼ tsp.	salt	1 mL
¼ tsp.	pepper	1 mL
1 tbsp.	onion	15 mL

Combine all ingredients and mix well. Season to taste. Shape into small balls and add to the sauce. Simmer for 2-2½ hours.

Serve hot over spaghetti or rice. Serves 4.

Lucille Le Lievre
St. Joseph du Moine, N.S.

Cape Breton Highlands
National Park

Jasper National Park

Alberta

Jasper National Park preserves one of the largest natural areas in North America. It offers expansive wilderness beauty and the richness of human history.

The park inherited its name from a trading post operator, Jasper Hawes. He established a trading post for the North West Company on the Athabasca River below the present townsite of Jasper. The supply depot became known as Jasper House. Over the years, the name Jasper was applied to the whole valley and eventually to the park itself, when it was established in 1907.

Jasper combines rugged peaks, luxuriant alpine meadows, icy lakes, bubbling hotsprings, broad forested valleys and grasslands, sand dunes, a river that disappears underground, and massive, awe-inspiring glaciers and icefields. The Columbia Icefield is one of North America's largest ice sheets, south of the Arctic Circle. The Athabasca Glacier flows from this Mammoth ice sheet and is always in motion flowing downward and forward. You can see firsthand how the movement of these glaciers, over the centuries, have carved the landscape. For those who have dared to challenge this mountain wilderness, solitude and superlative scenery have been the rewards for surviving a harsh environment.

Because of the severity of the area, few Indians roamed through these valleys. But a surprising variety of explorers chronicled the hardships encountered here. David Thompson slogged over the Athabasca Pass in 1811 in seven feet of wet cumbersome snow. It was not until 1892 that Lewis Swift, an adventurer from Ohio, became the first settler. Swift and his brood of children raised a variety of produce with a combination of tender loving care and an irrigation system supplied by a wooden water wheel. Before the establishment of the park, they supplemented their diet with wild herbs, berries, and big game. Lewis Swift became one of the first park wardens.

Another significantly important explorer was Mary Shäfter who came from a surprising background. She was a Philadelphia socialite! She diligently explored the Maligne Lake Country in 1908 revealing a spectacular gorge, the deeply gouged Maligne Canyon and the brilliant beauty of glacial fed Maligne Lake.

Much of Jasper National Park is still untouched wilderness and you can experience the same thrills that early explorers savoured as you meander the extensive back-country trails.

Terra Nova Meatballs

MEATBALLS

1 lb.	ground beef	500 g
½ cup	wheat germ	125 mL

Combine ground beef and wheat germ. Shape into balls and place on a baking sheet. Bake for 10-15 minutes at 350°F (180°C).

SAUCE

14 oz.	can pineapple tidbits	398 mL
⅓ cup	vinegar	75 mL
½ cup	brown sugar	125 mL
2 tbsp.	cornstarch	30 mL
½ cup	green pepper, chopped	125 mL

Drain pineapple juice into a small saucepan. Set pineapple chunks aside for later.

Add vinegar, brown sugar, and cornstarch to the pineapple juice. Heat over low heat until thickened. Add green pepper and pineapple chunks.

Place meatballs into a 2 quart (2 L) casserole dish. Pour sauce over top and bake for 10-15 minutes at 350°F (180°C) or until heated through.

A very easy meal to prepare. It takes about 40 minutes from start to finish. Serves 4.

Madonna Moss
Eastport, Nfld.

Terra Nova
National Park

Waikiki Meatballs

1½ lbs.	ground beef	750 g
⅔ cup	cracker crumbs	150 mL
⅓ cup	minced onion	75 mL
1	egg	1
1½ tsp.	salt	7 mL
¼ tsp.	ginger	1 mL
¼ cup	milk	50 mL
1 tbsp.	shortening	15 mL
2 tbsp.	cornstarch	30 mL
½ cup	brown sugar (packed) or	125 mL
1 tbsp.	sugar substitute	15 mL
14 oz.	can pineapple tidbits	398 mL
⅓ cup	vinegar	75 mL
1 tbsp.	soy sauce	15 mL
⅓ cup	green pepper, chopped	75 mL
10 oz.	can mushrooms (optional)	284 mL

Combine beef, crumbs, onion, egg, salt, ginger, and milk, and mix thoroughly. Shape mixture by rounded tablespoonfuls into balls.

Melt shortening in a large skillet. Brown and cook meatballs. Remove meatballs from skillet and keep warm. Pour fat from skillet.

Combine cornstarch and sugar and mix well. Stir in syrup from pineapple tidbits, vinegar, and soy sauce and blend until smooth. Pour into skillet and cook over medium heat, stirring constantly, until mixture thickens and boils. Boil and stir for 1 minute.

Add meatballs, pineapple tidbits, green pepper, and mushrooms. Heat through. Serves 6.

Irois and Annette Breau
Ste.-Marie De Kent, N.B.

Kouchibouguac
National Park

Potluck Party Casserole

6 oz.	wide noodles	170 g
2 lbs.	ground beef	1 kg
2 cups	onions, chopped	500 mL
2 tbsp.	butter	30 mL
1 cup	celery, chopped	250 mL
10 oz.	can mushroom soup	284 mL
10 oz.	can cream of chicken soup	284 mL
10 oz.	can mushrooms (including the liquid)	284 mL
1 cup	canned water chestnuts, sliced	250 mL
1 tbsp.	Worcestershire sauce	15 mL
¼ tsp.	salt	1 mL
¼ tsp.	pepper	1 mL
1 cup	Cheddar cheese, grated	250 mL

Boil noodles according to package directions. Drain and rinse with hot water.

In large frying pan, sauté beef and onions in 2 tbsp. butter. When beef is brown, add celery, soups, mushrooms, water chestnuts, and Worcestershire sauce. Season to taste.

Turn mixture into a greased 2 quart (2 L) baking dish, and top with grated cheese. Bake for 35 minutes at 350°F (180°C), until lightly browned. Serves 8.

Elaine Milne
Honey Harbour, Ont.

Georgian Bay Islands
National Park

Grandma's Birthday Lasagna

1 lb.	ground beef	500 g
½ cup	onion, chopped	125 mL
1	clove garlic, finely chopped	1
1	large green pepper, chopped	1
15 oz.	can tomatoes or nearly 2 cups	500 mL
6 oz.	can tomato paste	180 g
1 cup	water	250 mL
10 oz.	can button mushrooms	284 mL
1¼ tsp.	salt	6 mL
¼ tsp.	pepper	1 mL
1 tsp.	oregano	5 mL
¼ tsp.	chili powder	1 mL
½ lb.	lasagna noodles	250 g
1 tbsp.	oil	15 mL
2 cups	grated mozzarella cheese	250 mL
2 cups	cottage cheese	250 mL
¼ cup	grated Parmesan cheese	50 mL

In a very large frying pan or saucepan, brown the meat lightly, breaking it up as it browns. Add onion, garlic, and green pepper and sauté gently for 2 minutes. Add tomatoes, tomato paste, water (using it to rinse out tomato paste can), mushrooms, salt, pepper, oregano, and chili powder. Simmer 45 minutes uncovered.

Boil noodles in 3 quarts boiling water and 1 tbsp. (15 mL) oil for 15 minutes. Drain through a colander.

Have ready a large shallow 13"x 9"x 2" (33 cm x 23 cm x 5 cm) baking dish. Cover bottom with ⅓ of the noodles. Cover them with ⅓ of the meat sauce, and ⅓ of each of the cheeses. Repeat these 3 layers.

Bake for ½ hour at 375°F (190°C). Serves 8.

Florence Willoughby
Regina, Sask.

Riding Mountain
National Park

We often celebrate birthdays at Clear Lake. The best present of all is this delicious dinner treat!

Chili Con Carne

2 lbs.	ground beef	1 kg
2	large onions, chopped	2
¼ tsp.	salt	1 tsp.
¼ tsp.	pepper	1 tsp.
½-1 tsp.	garlic powder (to taste)	2-5 mL
19 oz.	can spagetti sauce	570 g
2 - 10 oz.	cans tomato soup	2 - 284 mL
5½ oz.	can tomato paste	156 mL
2 - 19 oz.	can kidney beans, drained	2 - 570 g
1	green pepper, chopped	1
1½ cups	mushrooms, sliced	375 mL
14 oz.	can olives	398 mL
1-2 tbsp.	chili powder (to taste)	15-30 mL
½ tsp.	paprika	2 mL
½ tsp.	oregano	2 mL
2 tbsp.	molasses (the secret!)	30 mL

Brown the beef in a skillet or in an electric frying pan. Pour off the fat. Add the onions and brown for about 2 minutes. Season with salt, pepper, and garlic.

Add all the remaining ingredients. Stir well. Simmer on low heat for about 45 minutes, stirring occasionally. Serves 8-10.

Steve Godfry
Ontario

Georgian Bay Islands
National Park

Steve's secret ingredient is molasses! It provides a taste treat you won't want to miss!

Elk Island National Park

Alberta

How can you have an island in the middle of the prairie? Well, Elk Island National Park is certainly not an islet in the usual sense of the word. However, it is insular in several respects.

First of all, it is an island in terms of its geological history. It stands as an intrusion on the surrounding plain. The landscape consists of water-filled hollows or kettle ponds and rolling hills or knobs. These "knobs" and "kettles" were formed by retreating glaciers 10,000 years ago. At the tips of the glaciers, big chunks crumbled off, leaving glacial debris surrounding these mounds of ice. The debris formed the knobs that we see today and the ice eventually melted to form kettle ponds.

This area has, for centuries, also formed an island of preservation. Natives sought protection here from bitter, prairie, winter winds and relied on the plentiful food supply in this secure environment.

The aggresive competition of fur traders and the arrival of early settlers firmly established man's presence in the surrounding area. As man sternly affirmed his supremacy on the prairies, species such as the bison and the beaver became unjustifiably depleted. In response to this, Elk Island became an isle of sanctuary for animals whose existence became threatened by advancing settlement. Here the waterfowl rest in peace, herds of elk roam freely and plains bison graze lazily, sheltered from the encroachment of man.

This prairie oasis offers a leisurely contrast from the fast pace of frantic urban living. Here there is time . . . time to soak in the sparkling glimmer of a dusky rose sunset or to gaze thoughtfully as a duck family ripples peacefully by. You can, also, patiently spy on an industrious beaver as he labouriously constructs his complicated dam.

Today, this national park provides a fenced island refuge which transports you away from life's problems. Here, the wildlife, the landscape, and the history of the area are preserved, to be enjoyed in an atmosphere of timeless tranquility.

Elk Island National Park

Spaghetti Sauce Supreme

1 tbsp.	corn oil	15 mL
1 lb.	lean ground beef	500 g
¼ cup	water	50 mL
1 tsp.	rosemary	5 mL
1 tsp.	tarragon	5 mL
1 tsp.	savoury	5 mL
1 tsp.	marjoram	5 mL
1 tsp.	ground thyme	5 mL
1 tsp.	chili powder	5 mL
½ tsp.	black pepper	2 mL
¼ tsp.	dill salt	1 mL
1	small whole garlic, very finely chopped OR	1
1 tsp.	garlic powder	5 mL
1	medium green pepper, finely chopped	1
1	medium onion, finely chopped	1
1	stalk celery, chopped	1
13 oz.	tin tomato paste	369 mL
¾ cup	good red wine	175 mL
1 cup	shredded cheese (½ Swiss, ½ old Cheddar)	250 mL
½ lb.	mushrooms or 10 oz. tin (284 mL) spaghetti boiling water	250 g
1 tsp.	vegetable oil	5 mL
½ tsp.	salt	2 mL

You may use a large frying pan or pot. (Heavy aluminum or steel is best. If you have a cast-iron pot, you can use it but remember the tomato is very acidic and may not be good for your cast-iron.) We use an electric frying pan.

Heat the pan to 450°F (230°C) and add the corn oil. Put the hamburger in the pan and break it up very finely. Sear the meat completely. This takes about 2 minutes. Add water, spices, and vegetables. Do not add the mushrooms at this time. Reduce the heat to 275°F (140°C) and let it simmer for 10 minutes.

After 10 minutes add your tomato paste and wine. Mix thoroughly and let simmer for another 10 minutes. Then add the cheese and mushrooms. Reduce the heat to 225°F (110°C) and let simmer for a further 10 minutes. The sauce is then ready. It will make enough for about 8 average eaters. We find it enough for at least 2 meals for 3. It keeps very well in the refrigerator. In fact, it improves with age!

We use spaghetti with egg in it. (There are several kinds on the market.) It should be cooked to desired texture, in boiling water to which oil and salt have been added. Drain well and wash under hot water before serving.

The sauce is very thick and can be thinned with either water or wine to suit your taste.

Keith Dewar
Smiths Falls, Ont.

St. Lawrence Islands
National Park

"Chiar" de Goelette (Gaspesie)

Fry a pound of sliced salted pork in a heavy frying pan. Fry until golden brown. Remove the lean pieces.

Add brown sugar and chopped onions to the grease. Brown. Add sliced potatoes and water. Season to taste and cover. Simmer until done. Serve with pork.

The origins of this recipe date back to 1895. During sailing expeditions, fishermen only carried salt pork, onions, and potatoes on their voyages to Québec to sell their fish.

Aline Jalbert
Québec

Forillon
National Park

"Chiar" de Goelette (Gaspésie)

Dans un chaudron de fonte, déposer une livre de lard salé coupé en tranches. Laisser cuire jusqu'à ce que les grillades soient dorées et croustillantes. Retirer alors les grillades.

Dans la graisse fondue, ajouter un tout petit peu de cassonade et de gros oignons tranchés. Laisser dorer. Ajouter alors des patates en tranches et de l'eau pour couvrir. Saler, poivrer et ajouter quelques herbes salées. Laisser mijoter doucement.

Servir avec les grillades de lard salé.

Pourquoi ce nom "Chiar de goélette"? Lors de la navigation, vers l'an 1895, les pêcheurs n'apportaient avec eux que lard salé, oignons et patates sur les goélettes, pour aller vendre le poisson salé à Québec.

Aline Jalbert
Québec

Forillon
National Park

Chinese Pie

1	small onion, chopped	1
½	green pepper, chopped	½
1 tbsp.	butter	15 mL
2 lb.	hamburger	1 kg
6	potatoes	6
¼ cup	milk	50 mL
¼ tsp.	salt	1 mL
⅛ tsp.	pepper	0.5 mL
1 tbsp.	butter	15 mL
14 oz.	can creamed corn	398 mL
1 tsp.	parsley flakes	5 mL

Sauté onions and green pepper in 1 tbsp. (15 mL) butter. Add hamburger and brown. Drain off any fat.

Peel and boil potatoes. Mash and add milk, salt and pepper, to taste, and 1 tbsp. (15 mL) butter.

Place hamburger mixture in 2 quart (2 L) casserole dish. Cover with creamed corn. Cover corn layer with mashed potatoes. Sprinkle parsley on top.

Bake for 30 minutes or until potatoes begin to brown at 350°F (180°C). Serves 6-8.

J. J. Williams
Ingonish Beach, N.S.

Cape Breton Highlands
National Park

Ham Sauce

¼ cup	tomato soup	50 mL
¼ cup	sugar	50 mL
¼ cup	vinegar	50 mL
¼ cup	butter	50 mL
¼ cup	prepared mustard	50 mL

Combine all the ingredients in a saucepan. Stir over medium heat for about 3-5 minutes. Store in the refrigerator. This is a lovely accompaniment with baked ham! Makes about 1 cup of sauce.

Emma Ringstrom
Winnipeg, Manitoba

Riding Mountain
National Park

Emma and her husband bought the Wasagaming Lodge Hotel in Riding Mountain National Park in 1968. Since that time Emma has written numerous articles about the park and is author of "Riding Mountain, Yesterday and To-Day."

SEAFOOD

Crêpes Delice de Mer

Keltic Lodge

CRÊPES

2	eggs	2
½ tsp.	salt	2 mL
1 cup	flour	250 mL
1 cup	milk	250 mL
1½ tbsp.	melted butter	25 mL

Combine eggs and salt in a bowl. Beat at medium speed. Gradually add the flour alternately with the milk until the mixture has a smooth consistency. Add the melted butter while continuing to beat. Let the mixture stand for 1 hour.

Heat a 6" (15 cm) greased frying pan. Pour ¼ cup (50 mL) of the batter into the pan. Cook until golden brown on both sides. Stack crêpes on a plate.

FILLING

4 tbsp.	butter	60 mL
2 tbsp.	shallots or onions, finely chopped	30 mL
½ lb.	sliced fresh mushrooms	250 g
¼ tsp.	salt	1 mL
⅛ tsp.	pepper	0.5 mL
3 cups	combination of cooked lobster, crab meat, scallops, shrimp, and clams	750 mL
4 cups	Thermidore Sauce (recipe follows)	1 L
½ cup	Parmesan cheese, grated	125 mL

Heat butter to bubbling and sauté shallots or onions and sliced mushrooms until limp but not brown. Add salt and pepper to taste and 1 cup of the Thermidore Sauce. Add seafood and mix well.

Put a spoonful or 2 of filling down the centre of each crêpe. Roll up and place them seam side down in a buttered 9" x 13" (23 cm x 33 cm) baking dish. Top crêpes with remaining sauce and sprinkle Parmesan cheese on top. Bake for 20 minutes at 375°F (190°C).

THERMIDORE SAUCE

6 tbsp.	butter	90 mL
6 tbsp.	flour	90 mL
3 cups	milk	750 mL
½ cup	white wine	125 mL
2 tbsp.	Dijon mustard	30 mL
1 cup	Cheddar cheese, grated	250 mL
¼ tsp.	salt	1 mL

Melt the butter in a saucepan. Blend in the flour. Gradually stir in the milk. Add wine and mustard. Cook and stir over medium heat until mixture comes to a boil and thickens. Remove from heat. Add the cheese and stir until melted. Salt to taste.

Serves 8-10.

M. Laroche
Keltic Lodge, Ingonish Beach, N.S.

Cape Breton Highland
National Park

Clam Stew Casserole

2 - 5 oz.	cans clams	2 - 142 g
1	small onion, diced	1
3	potatoes, diced	3
⅛ tsp.	nutmeg	0.5 mL
6	slices bacon	6
3 cups	milk	750 mL
¼ cup	butter	50 mL
¼ tsp.	salt	1 mL
⅛ tsp.	pepper	0.5 mL
⅛ tsp.	nutmeg	0.5 mL
1 tbsp.	chives, chopped	15 mL

Drain clams, saving the juice. Pour 1 cup (250 mL) juice into a small saucepan. Add onion and potatoes. Cook 10 minutes.

Dice bacon and brown. Put bacon, potatoes, onions, clams, and clam juice into a deep 2 quart (2 L) casserole. Add remaining ingredients.

Bake, covered, for 15 minutes at 325°F (160°C). Serves 4-6.

Delores Neal
Ingonish, N.S.

Cape Breton Highlands
National Park

Southern Creamed Shrimp

2 lbs.	raw shrimp	1 kg
	or	
1 lb.	cooked shrimp	500 g
4 tbsp.	butter, melted	60 mL
1 cup	celery, chopped	250 mL
½ cup	green pepper, chopped	125 mL
1 tsp.	onion, grated	5 mL
4 tbsp.	flour	60 mL
2 cups	cereal cream	500 mL
¾ tsp.	salt	3 mL
⅛ tsp.	curry powder	0.5 mL
1/16 tsp.	cayenne pepper	0.25 mL
2 tsp.	Worcestershire sauce	10 mL
1 cup	bread crumbs	250 mL
¼ cup	grated Parmesan cheese	50 mL

If using raw shrimp, steam cook for 2 minutes. Remove steamer from stove and let shrimp cook for 2 minutes longer. Remove shells.

Melt the butter and sauté the celery, green pepper, and onion until tender. Stir in the flour. Gradually add the cream, stirring until it comes to a boil. Add the shrimp. Season with salt, curry powder, cayenne pepper and Worcestershire sauce.

Place the shrimp mixture in individual dishes or a 1½ quart (1.5 L) casserole. Cover with the breadcrumbs and sprinkle with Parmesan cheese. Bake for 30 minutes at 425°F (220°C) or until bubbly. Serves 4.

Dorothy Parker
Yorkton, Sask.

Riding Mountain
National Park

Kluane National Park

Yukon

If you were limited to using one word to describe Kluane National Park, the word would be ICE. More than half of the park is covered by the spectacular mile-deep central icefields and imposing glaciers. These massive fields are fed by frequent snowstorms blowing in from the stormy Gulf of Alaska creating a formidable no man's land where only the legendary ice worm is a permanent resident.

These glaciers are actively carving and shaping the young rugged terrain. They currently cut, grind, and tear their way to lower levels, tangibly illustrating the process of glaciation. Most glaciers travel very slowly. However, some of these glaciers flow at astonishing rates and are known as "surging glaciers". During the 1960's, the Steele Glacier ground 11 km. downhill in only four months, giving rise to the nickname, the "Galloping Glacier".

In the midst of this perpetual winter landscape loom the youngest mountains in Canada. The towering summit of Mt. Logan is the highest peak in the country. These elusive slopes provide a sometimes dangerous but irresistible challenge for skilled mountaineers. They also elicit a quiver of excitement in a very real sense! This is the most earthquake-prone area in Canada and averages 1,000 tremors a year.

The extreme climate and variable topography has precluded settlement in the area. Early man crossed the Bering land bridge but wisely wandered south as the glaciers receded. Centuries later, the Southern Tutchone Indians began hunting, fishing, and trapping in harmony with the Kluane area. The northern silence of the land was later intruded and ravaged by greed, as fortune seekers were lured to the region when gold was discovered on Sheep and Bullion Creeks in 1903.

Although most of the park is a frozen ice-covered land, in the warmth of the lower valleys, the glaciers melt, giving birth to the major rivers of Kluane. The dryer and warmer ranges on the periphery of the icefields provide a home for one of the largest subspecies of moose in North America. Mountain goats freely climb the steep faces of the frontal ranges and the world's largest herd of snow-white Dall sheep feed on the moss-green alpine grasses, high among the mountain peaks. Great grizzly bears regally roam the park undisturbed.

This land of white-blue ice and mountain is so unique that it became, along with Wrangell-St. Elias National Park in the United States, the first jointly nominated World Heritage Site.

Everybody's Favourite Seafood Casserole

2 lbs.	fish, fresh, frozen, or canned (use a combination of scallops, lobster, haddock, shrimp, cod, or crab)	1 kg
2 cups	water	500 mL
2	chicken bouillon cubes	2
6 tbsp.	butter	90 mL
6 tbsp.	flour	90 mL
1 cup	Cheddar cheese, grated	250 mL
2	egg yolks	2
1 cup	cereal cream	250 mL
1 cup	mushrooms, sliced	250 mL
1 tbsp.	butter	15 mL
½ tsp.	Worcestershire sauce	2 mL
⅛ tsp.	cayenne pepper (optional)	0.5 mL
3 cups	bread cubes	750 mL
2 tbsp.	melted butter	30 mL

Thaw frozen fish and cut into cubes. (Individually frozen scallops and shrimp do not need to be thawed. Cut scallops in half.)

Cut lobster meat and fish fillets into bite-size pieces. Remove the cartilage from crab meat and check for shells. If using canned fish, drain and reserve the liquid.

In a large saucepan, boil 2 cups (500 mL) water. Add raw fish and simmer 3-4 minutes. Remove fish with slotted spoon and set aside. Pour reserved liquid from canned fish into a large measuring cup. Add enough stock, from boiling the fish, to equal 2 cups (500 mL). Add 2 chicken bouillon cubes and stir until dissolved.

Heat butter in the top of a double boiler. Stir in flour and cook for several minutes. Gradually beat in the 2 cups (500 mL) of hot liquid. Continue to cook, stirring constantly until the sauce thickens. Add cheese and stir until melted. Remove from heat.

Combine egg yolks and butter. Beat with a fork and slowly add to the sauce, stirring constantly. Set sauce aside.

Sauté mushrooms in 1 tbsp. (15 mL) butter. In a 1½ quart (1.5 L) greased casserole, combine the fish, sauce, mushrooms, Worcestershire sauce, and cayenne. Taste and add salt if necessary.

Toss bread cubes in melted butter, and sprinkle on top. Bake at 400°F (200°C) about 15 minutes or until cubes are golden. Serves 4.

Doris Hatt
Alma, N.B.

Fundy
National Park

Salmon Loaf

1 tbsp.	gelatin (unflavoured)	7g
⅓ cup	cold water	75 mL
16 oz.	can salmon	500 g
1	loaf French bread	1
½ cup	Philadelphia cream cheese	125 mL
3 tbsp.	mayonnaise	45 mL
¼ tbsp.	dry mustard	4 mL
½ cup	chopped sweet pickle	125 mL
3 tbsp.	ketchup	45 mL
⅛ tsp.	pepper	0.5 mL
3 tbsp.	chopped pimiento (optional)	45 mL

Soak gelatin in cold water. Place over low heat. Stir constantly until gelatin dissolves.

Drain and remove bones and dark skin from salmon.

Cut off the end of the loaf of bread. Hollow out the inside, leaving approximately ½" (1.3 cm) of bread and crust on the outside. Break the bread removed from the loaf into soft crumbs. (This can be done in a blender or food processor.)

Combine salmon, crumbs, cream cheese, mayonnaise, mustard, pickle, ketchup, pepper, and pimiento.* Mix well. Add gelatin.

Fill loaf with salmon mixture, inserting a long-bladed knife occasionally to remove any air bubbles. Fasten the end of the loaf on with toothpicks or skewers. Wrap in waxed paper or foil wrap, and refrigerate for at least 8 hours. Slice to serve. Makes 10-15 slices.

*More ketchup may be used to add colour.

Gary Casey
Barnaby River, N.B.

Kouchibouguac
National Park

Freezing Crab Meat

Cook the crabs for about 20 minutes in boiling water. Once the meat has cooled a bit, clean the crabs out.

Place the crab meat in containers, about ¾ full. Add salt and water to taste. Freeze.

Diane Babineau
Richibucto Village, N.B.

Kouchibouguac
National Park

Piquant Scallops

1 lb.	scallops	500 g
¼ tsp.	salt	1 mL
¼ cup	fine dry bread crumbs	50 mL
3 tbsp.	butter	45 mL
1 tsp.	Worcestershire sauce	5 mL
2 tsp.	lemon juice	10 mL

Separate scallops and sprinkle with salt. Roll in bread crumbs. Arrange scallops in baking dish.

Melt butter. Add Worcestershire sauce and lemon juice. Pour sauce over scallops.

Bake in a hot oven, 450°F (230°C) for 15 minutes. Serves 4.

Marina Collins
Alma, N.B.

Fundy
National Park

Baked Stuffed Lobster

2	live lobsters [about 1 lb. (500 g) each]	2
	water	
	salt	
2 cups	soft bread crumbs	500 mL
2 tbsp.	butter, melted	30 mL
1 tbsp.	onion, minced	15 mL
⅛ tsp.	garlic salt	0.5 mL

You will need enough water to cover the lobsters. For each gallon of water, add ½ cup (125 mL) table salt. Bring water to a boil. Plunge lobsters, head first, into the boiling water. Cover the pot with a lid. When the water has returned to a boil, allow to simmer 5 minutes. Quickly cool lobster under cold water and drain.

Place lobster on its back. With a sharp knife or scissors, slit the lobster open on the underside from head to tail, being careful not to cut other shell. Remove stomach and sac which lies just back of the head. Remove dark intestinal vein running from stomach to tip of the tail.

Prepare bread dressing by combining crumbs, melted butter, onion, and garlic salt. Stuff dressing into the body cavities. Place lobsters on a 11½" x 7" (29 cm x 18 cm) baking pan. Bake for 15 minutes at 400°F (200°C). Serve with side dishes of melted butter. Serves 2.

Doris Hatt
Alma, N.B.

Fundy
National Park

St. Lawrence River Fish Rolls

4	hot dog buns	4
1 lb.	yellow river or lake perch, filleted	500 g
¼ cup	flour	50 mL
⅛ tsp.	pepper	0.5 mL
¼ tsp.	ginger	1 mL
1	small egg, beaten	1
3 tbsp.	corn oil or almond oil	45 mL
½ tsp.	lemon juice	2 mL
½ cup	of your favourite tartar sauce	125 mL
1	medium dill pickle or several sweet baby gherkins	1
4 tbsp.	good white wine	60 mL
1 tbsp.	corn oil	15 mL
1	large onion	1

Warm the buns in the oven. Mix the flour, pepper, and ginger. Dip fillets in beaten egg and dredge in flour mixture. Immediately put the fillets in a hot frying pan to which you have added the corn oil or the almond oil. Cook until tender and flaky. Add the lemon juice to the sauce that is forming in the pan just before you turn the fillets for the first time.

While the fish is cooking, take tartar sauce and add the finely chopped dill and the wine. Mix well.

In a separate hot skillet, heat the corn oil. When it starts to smoke, add the onion. The onion should be thinly sliced, not chopped. Cook until it begins to carmelize.

You're ready! Take a hot dog bun, put 2 or 3 fillets on it, add the onions and a tsp. of sauce. It may sound strange but it is really good!

Serves 2-4.

Note! Do not use ocean perch. We have also heard that it can be done with smelt but we have never tried it. The fish should be very fresh!

This is a traditional St. Lawrence River dish!

Keith Dewar
Smiths Falls, Ont.

St. Lawrence Islands
National Park

Poached Sole with Lobster

Dalvay-by-the-Sea

6-6 oz.	fillets of sole	6-170 g
2 cups	court bouillon (recipe follows)	500 mL
¾ lb.	cooked lobster meat	365 g
3 tbsp.	parsley, minced	45 mL
3 tbsp.	stale bread crumbs	45 mL
¼ tsp.	thyme	1 mL
¼ tsp.	salt	1 mL
⅛ tsp.	pepper	0.5 mL
2 cups	white wine hollandaise sauce (recipe follows)	500 m L
¼ cup	Parmesan cheese, grated	50 mL

Fold the fillets in half lengthwise. Tuck the ends underneath and arrange fish in a 9" x 15" (23 cm x 39 cm) flame-proof baking dish, just large enough to hold them in 1 layer.

Pour strained court bouillon over to half cover fish. Bring liquid to a boil over moderately high heat. Reduce heat to low and poach fish, covered with a buttered sheet of waxed paper, for 8 minutes. Pour off liquid.

Pick over the lobster meat and chop finely. Top the sole with the lobster, parsley, bread crumbs, thyme, and seasonings. Pour the hollandaise sauce over the fish and sprinkle Parmesan cheese on top. Put the fish under a preheated broiler, 4" (10 cm) from the heat. Broil until the top is golden brown. Serves 6.

Dalvay-by-the-Sea
P.E.I.

Prince Edward Island
National Park

See photograph page 96.

Court Bouillon

2 cups	water	500 mL
½ cup	dry white wine	125 mL
½	onion, chopped	½
1	whole clove	1
½	bay leaf	½
1 tbsp.	parsley, chopped	15 mL
1 tbsp.	carrot, chopped	15 mL
1 tbsp.	celery, chopped	15 mL
⅛ tsp.	thyme	0.5 mL

Combine all the ingredients in a saucepan, and bring to a boil. Simmer for 15-20 minutes. Strain the bouillon, retaining the liquid. Makes 2 cups. (500 mL)

White Wine Hollandaise Sauce

1 cup	butter	250 mL
6	egg yolks, beaten	6
½ cup	dry white wine (at room temperature)	125 mL
½ cup	boiling water	50 mL
3 tbsp.	lemon juice	45 mL
1/16 tsp.	cayenne pepper	0.25 mL

Melt the butter in the top of a double boiler over low heat. Slowly add the beaten egg yolks. Beat with a wire whisk until smooth.

Add the wine, boiling water, and lemon juice, beating after each addition. Sprinkle with cayenne and continue to beat and cook for 3-5 minutes until sauce thickens.

Cover and place over hot water until ready to use. (It should not stand too long.) If the sauce starts to curdle, beat vigorously with a rotary beater until smooth and creamy. Makes 2 cups. (500 mL).

Cod Fish Au Gratin

2 lbs.	cooked cod fillets	1 kg
3 tbsp.	butter	45 mL
4 tbsp.	flour	60 mL
2 cups	milk	500 mL
½ tsp.	salt	2 mL
⅛ tsp.	pepper	0.5 mL
1 cup	sharp Cheddar cheese, grated	250 mL

Flake fish and set aside.

Make a white sauce with butter, flour, milk, salt, and pepper. Stir until thick.

Arrange fish in the bottom of a greased casserole. Cover fish with the cream sauce and top with grated cheese.

Bake for 25-30 minutes at 350°F (180°C). Serves 4.

Margaret Fudge
Rocky Harbour, Nfld.

Gros Morne
National Park

Fiddlehead Broiled Mackerel

Keltic Lodge

	vegetable oil	
6-8 oz.	fresh mackerel fillets or frozen haddock fillets	180-250 g
⅛ tsp.	pepper	0.5mL
¼ tsp.	parsley	1mL
	Anchovy Butter (recipe to follow)	

Lightly grease a baking sheet with oil and lay the fillets skin side down. Season the fillets lightly with pepper, and turn skin side up.

Place in a preheated oven on low broil (to prevent the skin from burning). Broil for 5-10 minutes, until skin begins to blister. With a spatula, gently turn skin side down. Be careful not to break the fillets. Broil for about 5 minutes, or until done to your liking.

Top with a generous portion of anchovy butter and chopped parsley. Serve with lemon wedges, boiled potatoes, and fiddlehead greens.

Anchovy Butter

30	anchovy fillets	30
1 lb.	butter, softened	500 g

Pound the anchovy fillets to a paste, force them through a sieve. Work anchovy paste into the softened butter.

Form anchovy butter into a 1" (2.5 cm) round, pipe-like roll. Roll in wax paper and refrigerate. Cut into slices as needed. This can be frozen for 1 month.

Dismas Le Blanc
Keltic Lodge, Ingonish Beach, N.S.

Cape Breton Highlands
National Park

Nahanni National Park

Northwest Territories

This land of isolation and challenge is so exceptional, that in 1979 it had the honour of being the first natural area to be designated as a United Nations World Heritage Site. These special areas are protected under the UNESCO World Heritage Convention as natural sites of universal importance.

This secluded preserve is accessible only by air or by boat. The scenery is unsurpassed! There is the sparkling turbulence of Virginia Falls, the continent's most spectacular, undeveloped waterfall. It is twice the size of Niagara Falls! The water, shrouded in mist, plummets downward into tumultuous rapids and whirlpools as the South Nahanni River continues its vehement course, crashing through hairpin turns, swishing treacherously through narrow chutes, and careening through stark canyons. The secret to the winding energy of this defiant river is that its existence pre-dated the existence of the three mountain ranges that intersect it. In the lazy days of its early life, it wandered and twisted its whimsical way through the unresistent land. But as the earth folded, uplifting the mountains, the river cut down through the soft rock preserving its original path and offering challenge and exhileration to expert, adventurous canoers.

The South Nahanni River is also surrounded by legend. The promise of elusive gold lured prospectors to the bountiful river valleys. When the headless bodies of several of the adventurers were discovered, macabre names such as Deadman Valley and Headless Creek were attached to the area.

Another fascination is the Rabbitkettle Hot Springs. Its warm waters radiate outward, carrying minerals to the surface of the earth. Rapid cooling creates the intricately terraced mount of tufa rock or brightly coloured calcium carbonate.

There are secrets and wonders in this park that cautiously reveal themselves to audacious explorers. The marvels of the environment attract people from all over the world to this sequestered habitat.

Smelt Á la Pelee

Shake cleaned smelt in seasoned sifted flour.

Mix equal parts Aunt Jemima Pancake Mix and flat ginger ale to make a watery batter.

Dip smelt in batter.

Deep-fry smelt in hot oil (350-375°F) (180-190°C)

Serve and eat while hot.

P.S. For added variety try substituting beer for ginger ale.

The smelt, a slender, silvery fish, approximately 8"-10" long, was first introduced to the Great Lakes in 1912. Since that time it has realized a healthy population. Each spring as the water temperatures rise to 9 degrees C, the smelt begin to spawn in shallow sandy areas. Pelee's 12 miles of beaches provide the smelt with ideal spawning grounds.

"Smelting" has been a traditional family activity in the park since 1946. Each spring, approximately 25,000 fishermen, equipped with chest waders, nets and lanterns line 'Peleés' beaches in anticipation of the nightly run. The avid and amateur fishermen net, clean and fry thousands of these little fish during the annual run.

This recipe created years ago by "the unknown fisherman" has brought culinary delight to both park staff and visitors.

L. Meleg and J. L. Barlow
Leamington, Ont.

Point Pelee
National Park

Mouchetée Sautée à la Mauricienne

INGREDIENTS

> **trout**
> **flour**
> **salted lard**
> **smoked bacon**
> **strawberry jam**
> **tea**
> **frying pans**

Slice the salted lard into strips and boil to remove the salt. Fry the strips of lard. Fry the bacon. Collect the grease from the lard and bacon and combine into 1 frying pan. Coat the trout with flour. Fry the trout in the mixed bacon and lard grease. Eat with strawberry jam and a pot of tea.

According to one of the guides from the St. Bernard Club from St. Alexis des Monts, this is a typical recipe of the hunting and fishing clubs in the Mauricie region.

Nick Malone
St. Alexis des Monts, Qué.

La Mauricie
National Park

Mouchetée Sautée à la Mauricienne

TRUITE MOUCHETÉE

> **farine**
> **lard salé**
> **bacon fumé**
> **poêlons**
> **thé confiture de fraise**

Couper en tranches le lard et le bouillir pour le dessaler. Faire frire les tranches de lard. Faire frire le bacon. Récupérer led deuz graisses des deux fritures dans même poêlon. Rouler la truite dans la farine. Frire la truite dans la graisse. Déguster le tout avec confiture et bol de thé noir.

N.B. Recette typique des clubs de chasse et pêche de la Mauricie, d'après l'un des guides du club St. Bernard de St. Alexis des Monts.

Nick Malone
St. Alexis des Monts, Qué.

La Mauricie
National Park

Capilotade De Poisson
A Capilotade (Mixture) of Fish

Take some fish, roasted or fried, cut in pieces or slices; put it in a pot with butter, salt and a bit of cloves, orange peel, spices and large bread crumbs, green onion, some verjus or vinegar, and some capers, if you like, or some anchovies; boil it all together, then finish preparing the capilotade, remove the green onion, and grate a slice of bread and some nutmeg, if not already contained in the spices.

Le Cuisinier François, Paris, 1699, La Varenne

Capilotade de Poisson

Prenés du poisson roty, ou frit, coupé par morceaux ou trancons; mettez-le dans unplat avec du beurre, du sel, et un peu de clou, de l'écorce d'orange, de l'épisse, et de grosses chapleures de pain, une ciboule, du verjus ou du vinaigre, et des capres si vous en voulez, ou des anchois, faites bouillir tout ensemble, puis en dressant la capilotade, retirez la ciboule, et rapez de la croute de pain, et un peu de muscades s'il n'y en a point dans l'espisse.

Le Cuisinier François (1699)

Louisbourg, N.S.

La Forteresse de Louisbourg
Parc Historique National

Modern Version

1 lb.	cod fillets	500 g
2 tbsp.	butter	30 mL
¼ tsp.	salt	1 mL
⅛ tsp.	ground cloves	0.5 mL
1 tsp.	orange rind, grated	5 mL
⅛ tsp.	ginger	0.5 mL
2	green onions	2
⅓ cup	vinegar	75 mL
1 tsp.	capers or anchovies, minced (optional)	3
½ cup	dried bread crumbs, diced	125 mL
⅛ tsp.	nutmeg	0.5 mL

Fry the fillets for 8-10 minutes.

Place the fillets in a casserole with the remaining ingredients, except the bread crumbs and nutmeg. Cover and place in a hot oven, 400°F (200°C) for 10-15 minutes. When cooked, remove the green onion and sprinkle the bread crumbs and nutmeg on top.

Note: Verjus is an acid juice extracted from large unripened grapes. It is used like vinegar.

Hôtel de la Marine
Louisbourg, N.S.

Fortress of Louisbourg
National Historic Site

This recipe is part of the menu at the restored Hôtel de la Marine. The original proprieter in the 18th century was Pierre Lorant, a 35 year old fisherman. There were many cabarets in Louisbourg where there was rum or wine, lively conversation, and card games which helped provide entertainment to pass away the long, isolated evenings!

Fortress of Louisbourg National Historic Site

This walled town offered a unique blending. In the 18th century it was an urban centre which blended the traditions of Louis XV's France with the opportunities of the New World. The stately parlours of the rich stood beside the plain dwellings of the working poor. Magnificent buildings were erected alongside the harbour, which relied on trade and fishery. It was a place of peaceful living which experienced the ravages of war!

Even today, scientists are blending theory and fact to give us a picture of life during this era. Because of these efforts, we can now visit the Fortress of Louisbourg and touch the life of this romantic walled city in the summer of 1744.

Arctic Char Stew

1	arctic char	1
	water	
½ tsp.	salt	2 mL
4-5	carrots, chopped	4-5
2-3	potatoes, chopped	2-3
1	onion, chopped	1
13 oz.	can evaporated milk	369 mL
13 oz.	water	369 mL
2 tbsp.	flour	30 mL
¼ cup	water	50 mL
¼ tsp.	salt	1 mL
⅛ tsp.	pepper	0.5 mL

On top of the stove, put char in a large pot with enough water to cover. Add salt. Cook until barely tender. Drain, remove skin and bones. Flake the char. Combine flaked char and chopped vegetables in a large saucepan. Add milk and water. Cook for about ½ hour, or until vegetables are tender.

Combine flour and water, and add to the stew. Stir until thick. Add salt and pepper to taste. Serves 4.

Oleepa Karpik
Pangnirtung, N.W.T.

Auyuittuq
National Park Reserve

Maritime Clam Pie

2-5 oz.	cans clams	2-140 g
¼ lb.	diced bacon	120 g
5	medium potatoes, thinly sliced	5
2	medium onions, diced	2
1 tsp.	salt	5 mL
2 cups	clam liquid (from the 2 cans)	500 mL
½ tsp.	pepper	2 mL
	favourite pastry recipe	

Drain clams, rinse and reserve the liquid. Fry bacon until crisp.

In a greased 9" x 13" (4L) baking pan, layer ½ the potatoes, onions, clams, salt, and pepper. Repeat the layers. Sprinkle with bacon and the fat from cooking. Pour clam liquid over everything.

Bake for 1 hour at 325°F (160°C). Cover dish with pastry. Prick pastry to allow steam to escape. Continue to bake at 450°F (230°C) for 15 minutes, or until pastry is lightly browned. Serves 8.

Gilles Babin
New Brunswick

Kouchibouguac
National Park

Wood Buffalo National Park

Alberta and Northwest Territories

Wood Buffalo National Park is Canada's largest park and is also the second largest national park in the world. The park was established to protect the last remaining herd of Wood Buffalo. These bison are larger and darker than their southern relatives, the Plains Bison. The Wood Buffalo were first protected from hunting in 1893. At this time, about 500 of these majestic beasts remained and they had sought refuge in the area where the park is today. Shortly after the establishment of the park, approximately 6,600 Plains Bison from near Wainwright, Alberta, were transported by rail and by river to the reserve. The two species intermingled and now many of the 5,000-6,000 bison in the park may be hybrids. These buffalo form the largest free-roaming herd in existence. This herd, together with the wolves in the park, continue a predator-prey relationship that is thousands of years old.

The nesting place of the last remaining 21 whooping cranes in existence was discovered in 1954 in a remote section of the park. This is the only nesting site of wild whooping cranes in the world. As a result of intensive, but cautious, management of the breeding pairs protected within the park, the species is recovering. The flock now numbers 80 in comparison with a world population of 120.

The park also contains many important natural features including one of the largest inland deltas in the world. In its peaceful stillness, lie the largest, undisturbed grass and sedge meadows left in North America. This rich delta supports most of the park's bison herds, provides spawning grounds for goldeye, and is a staging area for hundreds of thousands of waterfowl.

Wood Buffalo National Park displays one of the best examples of karst terrain in North America. The mineral gypsum is being dissolved out of the bedrock producing intriguing examples of collapse, sinkholes, small caves, and sunken valleys. These shadow-filled nooks and crannies provide essential hibernation sites for bats and reptiles.

The salt springs, unique in Canada, emerge from the base of a low escarpment and flow across flat, open areas, dramatically affecting plants and animals. During dry years, salt mounds over a metre high form at the springs. This salt that precipitates around the springs has enhanced the diet of native peoples in the area, as well as early explorers, fur traders, missionaries, and settlers.

These natural features and the rare wildlife in Wood Buffalo National Park are thought to be of world value. And for this reason, the park has been named a World Heritage Site. This area is recognized as being irreplaceable and preserves some of the world's most precious possessions!

Salmon Quiche

CRUST:

3	processed Cheddar cheese slices	3
¾ cup	flour	175 mL
½ cup	butter or margarine	125 mL
	(if using margarine, add a little more flour)	

Break up cheese slices and mix well with the flour and butter. Use a food processor or a blender if you have one. Press into a 9" (23 cm) pie plate.

FILLING:

1 cup	scalded milk	250 mL
2 tbsp.	butter or margarine	30 mL
¼ cup	green onion, chopped	50 mL
7¾ oz.	can red salmon (reserve the liquid)	220 g
2 tbsp.	chopped parsley	30 mL
2 tsp.	dill weed	10 mL
4	eggs	4
2 tbsp.	dry sherry (optional)	30 mL

In a saucepan, scald the milk. (Bring it just to the boiling point, and then remove from the heat.) Let it cool while preparing the fish filling.

Sauté the onion in butter until tender. Flake the salmon into a bowl. Add the onions, parsley, and dill weed.

Beat the eggs with the reserved salmon liquid. Add sherry if desired. Gradually add the scalded milk while still beating. Add to the fish mixture. Mix well, and pour into the pie shell.

Bake for 45 minutes at 350°F (180°C). Let the pie set for 10 minutes before cutting. This quiche is delicious served hot or cold and it will freeze well. Serves 6.

NOTE: To double the recipe use:

2 - 7 ¾ oz.	cans salmon	2 - 220 g
	or	
1	15 oz. can salmon	450 g

Thelma Bolduc
Ottawa, Ont.

*Riding Mountain
National Park*

Nova Scotia Lobster Quiche

Keltic Lodge

PASTRY

1 cup	flour	250 mL
¼ tsp.	salt	1 mL
¼ cup	butter	50 mL
1½ tbsp.	vegetable shortening	23 mL
3 tbsp.	cold water (approx.)	45 mL

Sift the flour and salt into a mixing bowl. Add butter and shortening. Crumble ingredients with your fingers until it resembles corn meal. Add water and blend it quickly, using a tossing motion.

Form a ball, and roll into a circle ⅛" (3 mm) thick. Line a pie plate with pastry and bake for 5 minutes at 450°F (230°C). Cool.

FILLING

2	green onions	2
2	shallots	2
8 oz.	lobster meat (canned, frozen, or fresh)	250 g
2	medium tomatoes	2
4 oz.	white Cheddar cheese	120 g
4	large eggs	4
2 cups	light cream	500 mL
⅛ tsp.	white pepper	0.5 mL
⅛ tsp.	nutmeg	0.5 mL
	paprika	

Slice green onions and shallots. Dice lobster, tomatoes, and cheese into small cubes.

Beat eggs into large mixing bowl. Add cream and beat well. Add pepper and nutmeg.

When ready to cook the quiche, cover the pastry shell with lobster mixture. Pour egg mixture on top. Sprinkle with paprika.

Bake for 10 minutes at 450°F (230°C) and then reduce heat to 350°F (180°C). Bake for 15 to 20 minutes, or until knife inserted in the centre comes out clean. Serves 4-6.

Keltic Lodge
Ingonish Beach, N.S.

Cape Breton Highlands
National Park

Swiss Cheese and Crab Quiche

1	9" (23 cm) pie shell, unbaked	1
4 oz.	Swiss cheese, shredded	120 g
1 cup	fresh crab	250 mL
2	green onions, chopped	2
3	eggs, beaten	3
1 cup	light cream	250 mL
½ tsp.	salt	2 mL
½ tsp.	grated lemon peel	2 mL
¼ tsp.	dry mustard	1 mL
¹⁄₁₆ tsp.	ground mace	0.25 mL
¼ cup	sliced almonds	50 mL

Arrange cheese evenly over bottom of pie shell. Top with crab meat and sprinkle with green onions.

Combine eggs, cream, salt, lemon peel, mustard and mace. Pour evenly over crab meat. Top with sliced almonds.

Bake for 45 minutes at 325°F (160°C) or until set. Let stand at room temperature for 10 minutes before serving. Serves 6.

Carole Sheffield
Tofino, B.C.

Pacific Rim
National Park

Lemon Sour Cream Stuffing

2 tbsp.	butter	30 mL
½ cup	celery, diced	125 mL
¼ cup	onion, chopped	50 mL
¼ cup	sour cream	50 mL
2 tsp.	lemon rind, grated	10 mL
½ tsp.	salt	2 mL
½ tsp.	paprika	2 mL
2½ cups	soft bread crumbs	625 mL

Melt butter. Add celery and onions and sauté.

Combine sour cream, lemon rind, salt, and paprika. Stir in bread crumbs and mix well.

This is an excellent stuffing for a 2-3 lb. Erickson Rainbow Trout.

Stella MacLean
Alma, N.B.

Fundy
National Park

POULTRY
& GAME

Partridge Hens with Cranberry

Chateau Lake Louise

⅔ cup	cranberries, chopped	150 mL
2 tbsp.	sugar	30 mL
1 tsp.	orange peel, grated	5 mL
½ tsp.	salt	2 mL
⅛ tsp.	cinnamon	0.5 mL
3 cups	toasted raisin bread cubes	750 mL
¼ cup	melted butter	50 mL
4 tsp.	orange juice	20 mL
4	partridge hens or Cornish hens	4
	cooking oil	
¼ cup	orange juice	50 mL

Combine cranberries, sugar, orange peel, salt, and cinnamon. Add the bread cubes and mix well. Sprinkle with ½ of the melted butter and 4 tsp. orange juice. Toss to mix.

Rinse the hens and pat dry. Rub the cavities with salt, and stuff with cranberry mixture. Skewer the neck skin to the back. Tie the legs to the tail and tuck the wings under the back. Place breast side up on a rack in a roasting pan. Brush with oil and cover loosely with foil. Roast for 30 minutes at 375°F (190°C).

Combine ¼ cup orange juice with the rest of the melted butter. Baste the birds and continue roasting, uncovered, for 1 hour or until done. Baste once or twice with the orange juice mixture while roasting. Makes 4 servings.

Jaroslav Nydr, Executive Chef
Chateau Lake Louise, Lake Louise, Alberta

Banff
National Park

Prince Albert National Park

Saskatchewan

Prince Albert National Park is the legacy created for us by a massive ice sheet that gouged and bulldozed its way across the land a hundred thousand years ago, leaving glacial formations of all kinds. Most obvious are the big lakes, whose basins were dug during the ice sheet's ponderous advance, but, everywhere, the glacier's gift is visible in a soft rolling landscape whose special beauty is as subtle as it is captivating.

Time, unable to erase the evidence of glacial action, has instead, preserved eskers and moraines throughout the park. This tell-tale debris, as well as the thick blanket of glacial till reminds us of days beyond all memory.

The bequest continues as this quiet place of sumptuous beauty unpretentiously offers a valued commitment to conservation. The secluded sheltered, northwest corner of the park provides a nesting ground for approximately 7,000 rare white pelicans. It is believed to be one of Canada's largest colonies and is the only fully protected colony in the country.

These peaceful surroundings seem to inspire a commitment to nature and it was this atmosphere that encouraged Grey Owl to establish his home here. This unassuming figure dedicated his life to preserving the intrinsic value of our natural environment. His deep love for the Canadian wilderness echoes throughout the isolated forests of the park.

Grey Owl reached out to millions of city dwellers from his silent, serene refuge. His timeless message said, "You are tired with years of civilization and I come to offer you, what?...a single green leaf."

Now many years later, this park offers you that same green leaf...a wilderness retreat where you can live close to nature, treasuring this gift from the past.

Phyllo Chicken

¼ lb.	butter, melted	115 g
24	phyllo sheets	24
4	boneless chicken breasts, cut in half (8 pieces)	4
10 oz.	pkg. fresh spinach, washed	300 g
½ lb.	feta cheese	250 g
1 tsp.	dill weed	15 mL

Melt butter, spread on 1 phyllo sheet. Place another sheet on top, spread with butter. Place 1 more sheet of phyllo on top. Place 1 chicken piece in the middle of phyllo sheets. Put several spinach leaves on top of chicken. Crumble 1-2 tbsp. (15-30 mL) feta cheese on top, add a pinch of dill weed.

Fold phyllo to make an envelope around chicken. Spread melted butter on top. Repeat with the other pieces of chicken.

Place chicken packages on a greased cookie sheet. Bake for 20-25 minutes at 375°F (190°C) until lightly browned. Serves 6-8.

Linda Dinsdale
Vancouver, B.C.

Riding Mountain
National Park

Chicken and Mushrooms

⅓ cup	butter	75 mL
½ tsp.	rosemary	2 mL
2 tsp.	paprika	10 mL
1 tsp.	salt	5 mL
¼ tsp.	pepper	1 mL
3 lbs.	chicken, cut up	1.5 kg
¼ cup	flour	50 mL
½ cup	dry white wine	125 mL
2 cups	mushrooms, sliced	500 mL

Preheat oven to 375°F (190°C). Put butter in a 13" x 9½" x 2" (4 L) pan and place it in the oven until the butter melts. Remove pan from oven and stir in rosemary, paprika, salt, and pepper.

Roll chicken pieces in flour and arrange them in the baking pan. Bake 30 minutes, turning the chicken once.

Remove chicken from oven and add wine and mushrooms. Cover and bake for 30 minutes more or until tender. Serves 6.

Beth McKenzie
Calgary, Alta.

Riding Mountain
National Park

Giblotte

4-5	potatoes	4-5
14 oz.	can peas	398 mL
¼ cup	onions, to taste	50 mL
1 cup	cubed, cooked chicken	250 mL
10 oz.	can cream of celery soup	284 mL
1½-2 cups	milk	375-500 mL
¼ tsp.	salt	1 mL
⅛ tsp.	pepper	0.5 mL
	pie crust	

Peel potatoes, and cut into ½" cubes. Place in an 8" x 8" (20 cm x 20 cm) casserole. Add peas, onions (if desired), and chicken.

Spread soup on top. Add enough milk to cover potatoes. Add salt and pepper to taste.

Cover with pie crust. Cut small holes in the crust (vents).

Bake for 1 hour at 350°F (180°C).

This recipe was given to my mother by my grandmother and finally to me. It is very tasty. Serves 4.

Yves Bossé
St. Louis de Kent, N.B.

Kouchibouguac
National Park

Egg Rolls

DOUGH

2½ cups	flour	625 mL
1 tsp.	baking powder	5 mL
1 tsp.	salt	5 mL
½ cup	cold water	125 mL
1	egg, beaten	1

Combine flour, baking powder, and salt. Add cold water and beaten egg and stir until a dough is formed. Put dough in the refrigerator for 1 hour.

FILLING

4 cups	cabbage, finely chopped	1 L
6½ oz.	can chicken or tuna fish	195 g
½ cup	onion, finely chopped	125 mL
½ cup	celery, finely chopped	125 mL
½ tsp.	Accent	2 mL
1 tsp.	corn oil	5 mL
½ tsp.	salt	2 mL
½ tsp.	pepper	2 mL
1 tbsp.	soy sauce	15 mL
1	egg, beaten	1

Combine all the ingredients and mix well. Allow the mixture to sit for 20 minutes.

Roll out dough paper thin. Cut dough into 6" (15 cm) squares, and put 1 tbsp. (15 mL) of filling in the centre. Roll up, tucking in the ends. Dip in beaten egg, and deep-fry several at a time in hot fat. Fry egg rolls 2 minutes on each side. Makes approximately 12 egg rolls.

Shirley Clare
Alma, N.B.

Fundy
National Park

Wild Game and Game Birds

In these days of urban living, wild game and game birds are more or less a rarity. However, this is only a recent luxury! For 7,000 years or more, the inhabitants of this great wilderness relied on their skills as hunters for their survival. Each generation developed their own methods of obtaining and preparing food, but they all retained a respect for the land and depended on their relationship with the natural environment for their existence.

In recent years, this intrinsic relationship has been jeopardized and it has ultimately become necessary to set aside National Parks to preserve our precious wild game and game birds to ensure their existence for future generations.

The following recipes are included primarily for their historical significance. We are confident that game enthusiasts will look for the ingredients to these recipes in places outside our National Parks.

Braised Caribou

3 lbs.	roast of caribou	1.5 kg
6	slices bacon	6
3 tbsp.	fat	45 mL
1 tsp.	salt	5 mL
¼ tsp.	pepper	1 mL
1 cup	hot water	250 mL
1 tsp.	vinegar	5 mL
2	medium onions	2

Clean and wipe the roast well with a damp cloth.

Lard the caribou meat as follows: Pierce the caribou meat with a sharp narrow knife at 2" intervals. Push the slices of bacon into the holes.

Rub the outside of the roast with fat. Sprinkle with salt and pepper. Place roast in a roasting pan. Add the hot water, vinegar, and onion. Cover and cook on low heat (on top of the stove) for about 2 hours or bake 2 hours at 325°F (160°C).

Serves 4.

This recipe comes from an Inuit woman who lives in Pangnirtung which is near Auyuittuq National Park Reserve.

McNee's Mock Ham
(made with venison)

20 lbs.	venison	10 kg
2 tbsp.	saltpetre	30 mL
1 cup	brown sugar	250 mL
3 cups	coarse salt	750 mL
1 tbsp.	thyme	15 mL
2 tbsp.	salt	30 mL
1	large onion, chopped	1
1 tsp.	pepper	5 mL
1 tsp.	paprika	5 mL
4	bay leaves	4

Clean and remove the bones from venison. Place it in a large crock. Do NOT use a metal container. It must be a crock.

Dissolve saltpetre, brown sugar, and salt in 4 cups hot water. Pour over venison, adding more water to make enough liquid to cover venison by 2" or 3".

To keep venison under water, weigh it down with a plate on which a jar of water has been placed. Let venison cure 10 to 14 days in a cool place.

Rinse venison. Place venison in a large cooking pot. To keep venison from burning during the cooking period, place a grid or slat under the cooking vessel. Add seasonings and enough water to cover venison.

Cook, covered, on medium heat for 3 or 4 hours. Check it frequently, adding more water if necessary. (Meat should be covered with water at all times).

Remove from heat, and allow it to cool in its own juices. Serve hot or cold.

When "mock ham" is cooled, it may be made up into meal-size portions, placed in airtight plastic bags, sealed and frozen. Makes 20 lbs. (10 kg) Mock Ham.

Mary McNee
Brandon, Man.

Riding Mountain
National Park

Riding Mountain National Park

Manitoba

For some, the name of this park seems wishful thinking! However, this land mass towers above the rest of the landscape, a mosaic of forest shade, prairie sun and lake blue. For the first explorers, it was certainly a mountain in the context of the prairies. During these early years, horseback riding was the easiest method of penetrating these rugged heights in search of fur or game. So, these protrusions became known as the Riding Mountains. This highland plateau, lying in the centre of the North American continent, is a meeting place. Plant and animal communities from the north, south, and west converge to create some of the greatest natural diversity in Canada.

The park is a mingling of past and present. Centuries ago, native peoples found security and bounty in these rich environs. The last of their lineage still lie in a secluded cemetery on the shores of Clear Lake. No experience is comparable to the subtle merging of past and present as the northern lights overwhelm you on a silent, evening stroll through this historic cemetery.

In more recent years, Riding Mountain became a valuable source of building timber for the settlers in the surrounding communities. These forest resources also alleviated hardships for rural municipalities during the depression and World War II. Wood, cut by the German prisoners-of-war interned at White-water Lake in the park, was also sent to urban centres to help combat the shortage of fuel during this time. Saw dust piles, milling debris, fallen pasture fencelines, a network of bush trails and a herder's cabin fading in the sun are all that is left to recall these settlements of earlier days!

Riding Mountain National Park is a synthesis of diverse natural elements. In 1980 the east side of the park was devastated by fire. A fierce battle was waged for weeks to finally subdue this wilderness threat. Under watchful eyes, this charred landscape is experiencing the process of rebirth, a living lesson of the resiliency and regenerative forces that sustain our wilderness.

In this park, you can touch the silent serenity of a Clear Lake sunset as a lonely loon echoes in the distance, or in contrast, you can absorb the tenuous violence of a prairie thunderstorm. This oasis on the prairie landscape offers the opportunity to experience natural phenomena on many levels.

Rabbit Stew

2	rabbits	2
¼ cup	oil or butter	50 mL
2	large onions, chopped	2
2	celery stalks, chopped	2
1 tsp.	salt or to taste	5 mL
½ tsp.	summer savory	2 mL
¼ tsp.	pepper	1 mL
12 cups	boiling water	3 L
2 cups	carrots, chopped	500 mL
2 cups	potatoes, chopped	500 mL
1 cup	turnip, chopped	250 mL
1 cup	cold water	250 mL
½ cup	flour	125 mL

Wash and cut up rabbit. Brown rabbit pieces in oil or butter, in heavy pot. Add onion, celery, salt, summer savory, and pepper. Add boiling water. Cover tightly and simmer for 2 hours. Stir and turn rabbit pieces occasionally.

Add vegetables and continue simmering until vegetables are tender. (About ½-¾ hour).

Mix flour and cold water to form a paste. Add to the stew slowly, stirring constantly until thoroughly mixed in. Cook until stew thickens. Serves 6-8 hungry persons.

Note: Rabbit is the common term in the Atlantic provinces for the wild snowshoe hare. Newfoundlanders prefer to snare their rabbits and wash only lightly after removing the skin and stomach. Mainlanders, I have found out, after living in New Brunswick for 11 years, prefer to shoot their rabbits so that they are well-bled. A great deal of time is spent cleaning and washing the rabbit. I guess they don't like hare in the stew!

Barry F. Spencer
Richibucto, N.B.

Kouchibouguac
National Park

Reindeer Emince

Banff Springs Hotel

DEMI-GLAZE

2 tbsp.	butter	30 mL
2 tbsp.	flour	30 mL
1	beef bouillon cube	1
1 cup	boiling water	250 mL
few drops	Worcestershire sauce	few drops
¼ tsp.	salt	1 mL
⅛ tsp.	pepper	0.5 mL

Melt the butter in a saucepan. Stir in the flour until blended.

Dissolve beef bouillon cube in water. Add bouillon, Worcestershire sauce, salt, and pepper to flour mixture. Stir until smooth. Bring sauce to a boil, stirring constantly. Simmer gently for 10-15 minutes.

REINDEER

2½ cups	reindeer meat (hip), thinly sliced	625 g
⅓ cup	butter	75 mL
3 tbsp.	onions, chopped	45 mL
5	mushrooms, sliced	5
2 cups	red wine	500 mL
1 cup	demi-glaze	250 mL
2 cups	whipping cream	500 mL
¼ tsp.	salt	1 mL
⅛ tsp.	pepper	0.5 mL
1 tbsp.	brandy	15 mL
1 tsp.	cranberry sauce	5 mL
5	puff pastry shells	5

Sauté reindeer meat in butter for 3-5 minutes. Remove meat from pan and set aside. Add onions and mushrooms to the pan, and sauté until onions are soft and translucent. Add red wine and demi-glaze. Cook over medium heat until liquid is reduced to half.

Return reindeer meat to the sauce and heat without letting it boil.

Whip the cream. Fold half of it into the meat and sauce. Add salt, pepper, brandy, and cranberry sauce. Fill 5 puff pastry shells with reindeer emince. Top off with remaining whipped cream. Serves 5.

Thinly sliced roast beef can be used as an alternative to reindeer meat.

M. Luthi
Banff Springs Hotel, Banff, Alberta

Banff
National Park

Curried Moose

1 lb.	moose meat	500 g
¼ cup	soy sauce	50 mL
¼ tsp.	salt	1 mL
⅛ tsp.	pepper	0.5 mL
28 oz.	can stewed tomatoes	840 g
⅓ cup	green pepper, diced	75 mL
⅓ cup	celery, diced	75 mL
⅓ cup	onion, chopped	75 mL
14 oz.	can whole mushrooms	398 mL
10 oz.	can tomato soup	284 mL
1 cup	water	250 mL
1 tsp.	curry powder	5 mL

Marinate moose meat overnight in the soy sauce. Cut meat into bite-size pieces.

Place meat in a roaster and sprinkle with salt and pepper. Bake for 45 minutes at 325°F (160°C).

Combine stewed tomatoes, green pepper, celery, onion, and mushrooms. Combine tomato soup with water and add to tomatoes. Pour tomato mixture over the pre-cooked moose. Add curry powder to taste.

Bake for approximately 1 hour more. Serve with wild rice, vegetable of your choice, and fresh rolls. Serves 4.

Madonna Moss
Eastport, Nfld.

Terra Nova
National Park

Pukaskwa National Park

Ontario

Pukaskwa National Park is a wild shore of an "inland sea". It officially opened in 1983 to permit access to the wild shore of the Canadian Shield with its ancient, rocky landscape. The inland sea bordering this shore is Lake Superior, the largest of the Great Lakes. Together the Shield and the Superior give this park a wild, awesome, and fascinating appeal!

It is a land of mystery and intrigue carved in ancient rock, wrinkled and worn through endless eons. The combination of granite rocks and the extrusions of volcanic lava present a rough, rugged landscape, broken by slopes and depressions, riddled with tiny lakes and clothed in shallow soils.

The captivating power and expanse of the lake unpredictably conceals the land in dense fogs and mists. Its icy crystal depths can rage with rain and violent storms or suddenly return to a sparkling calm. The Superior's arctic-like influence encourages rare arctic plants to eke out a meagre existence in these southern climes.

Concealed in this obscure wilderness are the haunts of moose, wolf, black bear, and woodland caribou as well as smaller animals who conceal themselves in the boreal woods. The white-water of the Pukaskwa and White Rivers awakens the wandering spirits in many hearts.

Upon some of Pukaskwa's cobble beaches are mysterious pit-like structures presenting one of life's infinite puzzles. Did shamans, the custodians of the Ojibway rites, come here to honour or appease the omnipowerful spirits of land, sea, and skies? These pits tease the imagination because no one knows when or why these structures were made!

Europeans first explored these northern shores of Lake Superior in the 17th century and were soon followed by voyageurs. Between break-up and freeze-up, the voyageurs penetrated into the heart of the continent. They travelled west to Ft. William laden with woven goods, ironware, and trinkets. On their return to Montreal, their bark canoes were ballasted with furs. Pukaskwa also captured the imagination of missionaries in search of converts, miners, traders, lumbermen, and trappers. Each had his day and, in time, each abandoned the wild and remote lands of Pukaskwa.

For today and the tomorrows to come, Pukaskwa National Park beckons to those who wish to unravel the mystery and intrigue of this elusive sample of Canadian Shield, northern forest, and Superior coastline.

Burgundy Buffalo

1 lb.	buffalo stewing meat	500 g
½ tsp.	meat tenderizer	2 mL
2 tbsp.	water	30 mL
1	tomato, chopped	1
1	green pepper, seeded and chopped	1
2	stalks celery, chopped	2
½ cup	burgundy or dry red wine	125 mL
1	clove garlic, or	1
¼ tsp.	garlic powder	1 mL
¼ tsp.	chili powder	1 mL
½ tsp.	thyme	2 mL
1 tsp.	parsley	5 mL
1	bay leaf	1
½ tsp.	tarragon	2 mL
½ tsp.	marjoram	2 mL
1	onion, diced	1
10-12	mushrooms, sliced	10-12
½ cup	burgundy or dry red wine	125 mL
1-2 tbsp.	flour	15-30 mL

Cut stewing meat into bite-size pieces. Sprinkle with meat tenderizer. Pierce pieces with a fork to allow the tenderizer to penetrate. Let meat sit for 5 minutes.

Combine water and meat in a frying pan, and brown the meat on high heat for about 5 minutes.

Add tomato, green pepper, celery, burgundy, and seasonings. Cook on medium heat for 5 more minutes.

Pour mixture into a casserole dish. Cook covered for 1½ hours at 250°F (120°C).

Remove from oven and add onion and mushrooms. Add another ½ cup burgundy and cook for another 10 minutes. Thicken gravy with flour. Serve over hot rice or noodles. Serves 4.

NOTE: The buffalo is now a rare species so we recommend that you use beef stewing meat and you can still try this delicious recipe!

At one time, teeming herds of magnificent buffalo thundered, victoriously across the prairie plains. Indian people such as the Blackfoot, Assiniboine, Gros Ventre, and the Sioux depended upon these versatile animals for their food, clothing, and shelter. The men valiantly hunted the buffalo with lances, bows, and arrows and the women, in the aftermath of the victory, butchered the game and dressed the hides.

Wood Buffalo
National Park

Fried Muskrat

1	muskrat	1	
1 tbsp.	salt	15 mL	
1 quart	water	1 L	
1	egg yolk	1	
½ cup	milk	125 mL	
1 tsp.	salt	5 mL	
½ cup	flour	125 mL	
4 tbsp.	cooking fat	60 mL	

Remove the fat, scent glands and white tissue inside each leg. Soak the muskrat overnight in 1 tbsp. of salt (15 mL) to 1 quart (1 L) water. Cut the muskrat into desired pieces.

Parboil for 30 minutes. Drain and wipe with a damp cloth.

Make a smooth batter by beating the egg and milk. Then add 1 tsp. salt (5 mL) and the flour.

Heat the fat in a heavy frying pan. Dip the meat in the batter, then sauté in the hot fat until brown. When brown, reduce the heat. Cover and cook slowly for 1½ hours.

Serves 2.

Fort St. James National Historic Park officially opened in 1977 and tells the story of the fur trade on the Pacific slope. The fort was founded in 1806 by Simon Fraser for the North West Company. It became the headquarters of a vast fur trading district in north central British Columbia called New Caledonia. The main food for the fur traders was smoked salmon and dried salmon. This diet became very monotonous in the course of a year.

This invariable repast combined with the isolation, hard work and severe winters earned Fort St. James the name "The Siberia of the Fur Trade". To relieve the monotony of their diet, the men trapped fresh meat. Beaver and muskrat provided an innovative and welcome variation to their bland menu.

Ken Green
Fort St. James, B.C.

Fort St. James
National Historic Park

Baked Turr (Seabird)

2	turrs (cleaned)	2
1	piece fat-back pork	1
4-5 cups	water	1-1.25 L
2	onions, sliced	2
½ tsp.	salt	2 mL
⅛ tsp.	pepper	0.5 mL

Put a slit in each side of the turr breast. In each slit, place a piece of fat-back pork. (This keeps the meat from drying out, and adds a nice flavour to the meat).

Put the turrs in a roaster. Add water, sliced onions, salt, and pepper. Cover and bake for 3 hours at 350°F (180°C). Check periodically to ensure that the birds do not boil dry. Remove the cover for the last hour to allow the birds to brown. Cover with pie crust if desired. Serves

Turr or Common Turr is a native migratory salt-water bird.

PIE CRUST

1½ cups	flour	375 mL
⅛ tsp.	salt	0.5 mL
2 tsp.	baking powder	10 mL
1 tbsp.	butter	15 mL
2-3 tbsp.	water	30-45 mL

Combine all the ingredients and mix to form a dough. Roll the dough out to ⅛" (3 mm) thick and spread it over the turrs. Brush with additional melted butter to prevent the top from becoming too hard. Bake for 15-20 minutes at 350°F (180°C), until golden brown.

Miriam Pike
Eastport, Nfld.

Terra Nova
National Park

BREADS

Cinnamon Buns —
Kelly's Bake Shop Original

BUNS

1 cup	milk	250 mL
⅓ cup	sugar	75 mL
2 tsp.	salt	10 mL
½ cup	shortening	125 mL
1 tsp.	sugar	5 mL
½ cup	lukewarm water	125 mL
1 tbsp.	active dry yeast	7 g
1	egg, beaten	1
4-4½ cups	all-purpose flour	1-1.125 L

Scald milk. Pour into a bowl and add sugar, salt, and shortening. Cool the mixture until it is lukewarm.

Dissolve sugar in lukewarm water. Add yeast and let stand 10 minutes. Combine lukewarm milk mixture, yeast mixture, and beaten egg. Stir well.

Add 2 cups (500 mL) flour and mix well. Add the remaining flour and mix. Turn the dough onto a floured board and knead for 10-15 minutes. Place the dough in a greased bowl and turn to grease the top. Cover, and let the dough rise for about 1 hour or until double in bulk. Take the risen dough and roll it into a rectangle that is ½" (1.3 cm) thick.

FILLING

2 tbsp.	melted butter or margarine	30 mL
2 cups	brown sugar	500 mL
1 tsp.	cinnamon	5 mL
½ cup	butter or margarine	125 mL

Brush the rectangle with 2 tbsp. (30 mL) melted butter.

Combine brown sugar, cinnamon, and ½ cup (125 mL) butter. Spread half the mixture on the rectangle. Roll the dough up like a jelly roll, and cut into 1" (2.5 cm) slices.

Grease a 9" x 12" (4 L) pan, and spread the other half of the cinnamon sugar mixture on the bottom. Place the dough slices, cut side down, in the pan. Cover and let them rise for 1 hour, or until double in bulk.

Bake for about 25 minutes at 400°F (200°C) or until lightly brown.

ICING

2 tbsp.	icing sugar	30 mL
½ tsp.	water	2 mL
few drops	vanilla	few drops

Combine icing sugar, water, and vanilla. Spread over buns while they are still hot. Makes 1½ to 2 dozen.

Miriam Kelly
New Brunswick

Fundy
National Park

See photograph page 16.

Quick Brown Bread

1 cup	boiling water	250 mL
1 tbsp.	butter	15 mL
1 tsp.	salt	5 mL
½ cup	oatmeal	125 mL
1 tbsp.	active dry yeast, or 1 yeast cake	7 g
¼ cup	lukewarm water	50 mL
1 tsp.	sugar	5 mL
½ cup	molasses	125 mL
2¾-3 cups	flour	675-750 mL

Combine boiling water, butter, salt, and oatmeal. Cool until lukewarm.

Dissolve the yeast and the sugar in lukewarm water. Allow it to sit for 5 minutes.

Add yeast to oatmeal mixture. Add molasses and about 2½ cups (625 mL) flour. Mix well.

Turn dough onto a floured board and knead in the remaining flour. Knead for 8-10 minutees. Form into a loaf. Place in a greased 8½″ x 4½″ (20 cm x 10 cm) loaf pan, and let it rise in a warm place for 1 hour. Bake for 45-60 minutes at 375°F (190°C). Makes 1 loaf.

Frances Armstrong
Alma, N.B.

Fundy
National Park

This bread is easy to make, and has a rich natural flavour!

See photograph page 16.

Old-Fashioned Porridge Bread

3 cups	boiling water	750 mL
2 cups	rolled oats*	500 mL
¼ cup	margarine or butter	50 mL
2 tsp.	sugar	10 mL
1 cup	lukewarm water	250 mL
2 tbsp.	active dry yeast	14 g
⅔ cup	table molasses	150 mL
4 tsp.	salt	20 mL
2½ cups	flour	625 mL
5-6 cups	flour	1.25-1.5 L

Pour boiling water over oats. Add margarine and stir until margarine melts. Let stand for 20 minutes, stirring occasionally.

Meanwhile, dissolve sugar in water. Sprinkle yeast over water and let it stand for 10 minutes. Then stir briskly with a fork.

Add molasses and salt to oat mixture. Cool to lukewarm. Add yeast to lukewarm rolled oats. (If the rolled oat mixture is too warm, it will kill the yeast.)

Beat in 2½ cups (625 mL) flour. Beat vigorously by hand or with an electric mixer. Then gradually beat in remaining flour with a spoon. Work in the last of the flour with a rotating motion of the hand.

Turn the dough onto a floured board and knead 8-10 minutes. Shape into a smooth ball, and place in a greased bowl, turning dough to grease the surface. Cover, and let rise until double in bulk (1½ hours.) Keep in a warm place.

Punch dough down and form into 4 loaves. Place in greased 8½" x 4½" (20 cm x 10 cm) loaf pans. Grease the tops, cover and let rise again until doubled, 1 hour.

Bake in a preheated oven at 400°F (200°C), for about 30-35 minutes or until done. Makes 4 loaves.

Lucille LeLievre
St. Joseph du Moine, N.S.

*Cape Breton Highlands
National Park*

*Instead of 2 cups (500 mL) rolled oats, 1½ cups (375 mL) rolled oats plus ½ cup (125 mL) barley or triticale flakes can be used. It gives an interesting flavour.

See photograph page 96.

Food Processor Millet Bread

2 tbsp.	brown sugar	30 mL
1 cup	lukewarm water	250 mL
1 tbsp.	yeast	7 g
1 cup	all-purpose flour	250 mL
¼ cup	powdered milk	50 mL
¼ cup	millet	50 mL
¼ cup	bran	50 mL
¼ cup	wheat germ	50 mL
3 tbsp.	margarine	45 mL
1¼ cups	whole-wheat flour	300 mL
2 tbsp.	all-purpose flour	30 mL

Dissolve sugar in water. Sprinkle yeast on top and let it sit for 10 minutes.

Insert a steel blade in your food processor. Add all-purpose flour, powdered milk, millet, bran, wheat germ, and margarine. Process for about 10 seconds, until mixture looks like cornmeal.

Add ½ of the yeast mixture. Process with 4 on/off turns.

Add the remaining yeast mixture and the whole-wheat flour. Process with 4 on/off turns. If dough seems a bit sticky, add 2 tbsp. all-purpose flour and run the machine for about 10-15 seconds, just until the dough forms a ball. Do not process too long.

Remove the ball and any excess dough which may be on the bottom of the machine. Shape the dough with your hands. Place it in a greased bowl. Turn once to grease the surface. Cover. Let it rise for about 1 hour, until double in bulk.

Punch down. Shape into a loaf and place into a greased 8½" x 4½" (20 cm x 10 cm) loaf pan. Cover and let rise for 1 hour or until double in size.

Bake for about 30-40 minutes at 375°F (190°C) or until done. Makes 1 loaf.

Anne Mense
Winnipeg, Man.

Riding Mountain
National Park

This is a quick and easy way to make bread.

See photograph page 96.

Nutritious Northern Bread

4 cups	warm water	1 L
4 tbsp.	vegetable oil	60 mL
4 tbsp.	molasses	60 mL
2 tsp.	sugar	10 mL
1 cup	warm water	250 mL
2 tbsp.	yeast	14 g
6 cups	all-purpose flour	1.5 L
6 cups	whole-wheat flour	1.5 L
4 tsp.	salt	20 mL
1⅓ cups	powdered milk	325 mL
1 cup	brown sugar	250 mL

In a large bowl, combine 4 cups water, vegetable oil, and molasses.

In a small bowl, dissolve sugar in 1 cup water. Add yeast. Stir and let sit for 10 minutes.

In a large bowl, combine flour, whole-wheat flour, salt, powdered milk, and brown sugar. Mix well.

Add 2 cups (500 mL) of the flour mixture to the liquid mixture. Mix well. Add yeast mixture and mix again. Gradually add the remining flour mixture.

Turn dough onto a floured board and knead for about 8-10 minutes. Place the dough in a greased bowl. Turn dough to grease the top. Cover with waxed paper and place in a warm location for about 1½-2 hours or until double in bulk.

Punch the dough down and shape it into 4 loaves. Place in 4 well-greased 8½" x 4½" (20 cm x 10 cm) loaf pans. Let the loaves rise until they are double in bulk.

Bake for about 35-40 minutes at 375°F (190°C). Turn the loaves out of the baking pans, and cool on wire racks. Slice, butter, and enjoy!

Tom and Nell Smith
Red Deer, Alta.

Wood Buffalo and Waterton Lakes
National Parks

Nell had always hesitated to try her hand at home-made bread. However, when they were transferred from Ottawa to Wood Buffalo National Park, the lack of fresh bread in the North West Territories prompted her to overcome her reluctance and give it a try. A friend provided her with a "no-fail" recipe that even a "nincompoop" could succeed with. This recipe started a weekly tradition of bread baking that carried her family through the "fresh bread drought" in Waterton Park as well. This recipe for Nutritious Northern Bread is Nell's modification of that recipe and is even easier than the original. It is so delicious that it will probably start some traditions in your family too!

See photograph page 96.

The Banff Centre

The National Parks have often provided the setting for cultural activities. What better atmosphere could you have than the Banff Centre nestled in the heart of the Canadian Rocky Mountains? This location has the effect of distancing you from urban distractions and pressures. It frees creative energies.

The Banff Centre is a community of artists living and working together in an environment which challenges and stimulates creativity and promotes excellence. It is one of Canada's most advanced conservatories of the arts.

The Centre offers summer and winter courses in such disciplines as Music, Visual Arts, Theatre Arts, Writing, and Publishing. The Banff Festival of the Arts provides professional performing experience and exhibiting opportunities for students. The newest major innovation is the Leighton Artist Colony. The colony consists of eight specially designed studios which are invitingly put at the disposal of the established artists so that they can enjoy uninterrupted surroundings where they can intensively perfect their work.

With these accomplishments, it is little wonder that the Banff Centre has become one of the most prominent communities for the training and promotion of artistic talents in Canada.

The Banff Centre
School of
Fine Arts

Dilly Health Bread

1 tbsp.	dry active yeast	7 g
¼ cup	water	50 mL
1 tbsp.	sugar	15 mL
1 tbsp.	margarine	15 mL
1 cup	creamed cottage cheese	250 mL
1 tbsp.	sugar	15 mL
1	unbeaten egg	1
1 tsp.	salt	5 mL
1 tbsp.	instant minced onion	15 mL
1 tsp.	dill weed	10 mL
¼ tsp.	baking soda	1 mL
2 cups	whole-wheat flour	500 mL

Soften the yeast in the lukewarm water. Add 1 tbsp. sugar and let the yeast sit for 10 minutes.

Melt the margarine in a saucepan. Add the cottage cheese to the margarine and stir over low heat for 1-2 minutes until lukewarm.

In a large bowl, combine the yeast mixture, cottage cheese mixture, 1 tsp. sugar, egg, salt, minced onion, dill weed and baking soda. Gradually stir in 1 cup (250 mL) whole-wheat flour, stirring after each addition.

Turn the dough onto a floured board. Knead in the remaining 1 cup (250 mL) flour. This should take about 8-10 minutes. Place the dough in a greased bowl and turn to grease the top. Cover the dough and let it rise for 50-60 minutes or until double in bulk.

Punch the dough down and place it in a greased 1 qt. (1 L) casserole dish. Bake for 40-50 minutes at 350°F (180°C). Be careful not to overbake it. Makes 1 loaf.

Norma Ferguson
Winnipeg, Man.

Riding Mountain
National Park

See photograph page 16.

Pizza Dough

DOUGH

1 tsp.	yeast	5 mL
1 tsp.	sugar	5 mL
¾ cup	lukewarm water	175 mL
2¼ cup	flour	550 mL
1½ tbsp.	vegetable oil	23 mL

Dissolve yeast and sugar in water. Let it stand for 10 minutes, then stir well.

Stir in flour and oil. Turn out onto a floured board. Knead for 8-10 minutes. Place in a greased bowl, turning to grease the top. Cover and let rise for about 40 minutes.

Punch down and press into a greased pizza pan or cookie sheet. This makes a thick crust. Top with your favourite toppings and bake for 25-30 minutes at 375°F (190°C).

Claudette Saquet
Wasagaming, Man.

Riding Mountain
National Park

Pizza Sauce

5½ oz.	can tomato paste	156 mL
1¼ cup	water	300 mL
1 tsp.	sugar	5 mL
1 tsp.	vegetable oil	5 mL
½ tsp.	chili powder	2 mL
1 tsp.	oregano	5 mL
⅛ tsp.	garlic	0.5 mL
½ tsp.	basil	2 mL
¼ tsp.	salt	1 mL
⅛ tsp.	pepper	0.5 mL

Combine all of the ingredients in a 4 cup (1 L) measuring cup, or a bowl with a spout. Mix well. Pour sauce onto pizza crust and spread evenly. Top with your favourvite toppings (e.g. salami, onions, ham, mushrooms, green pepper) and lots of grated mozzarella cheese.

This makes enough sauce for 1 pizza.

Anne Mense
Winnipeg, Man.

Riding Mountain
National Park

Bang-Belly

4 cups	homemade bread cubes [1" (2.5 cm) cubes]	1L
	water	
¾ cup	salt pork	175 mL
	OR	
½ cup	butter	125 mL
½ cup	molasses	125 mL
½ tsp.	cinnamon	2 mL
½ tsp.	allspice	2 mL
½ tsp.	cloves	2 mL
½ tsp.	baking soda	2 mL
1 cup	flour	250 mL
¾ cup	raisins	175 mL

Soak bread cubes in enough water to cover for 3-5 minutes, until the bread is soft. Drain well.

If you are using salt pork, cut it into small cubes. Combine salt pork or butter and drained bread cubes. Add molasses.

Combine the spices, baking soda, and flour and add to the bread mixture. Stir in raisins.

Pour into a greased 7½" x 3½" (20 cm x 10 cm) loaf pan. Bake for about 50 minutes at 300°F (150°C). When bang-belly cools, cut it into slices or squares. Makes 1 small loaf.

Mildred Powell
Eastport, Nfld.

Terra Nova
National Park

We used store-bought bread and butter instead of salt pork. It made a lovely moist loaf!

One doesn't very often associate pirates with our National Parks! However, the scoundrel, Peter Easton, threatened the shores near Terra Nova National Park. His notorious career involved sailing into Conception Bay and attacking John Guy's colony at Cupids, keeping Richard Whipbourne captive for 11 weeks. He also threatened the communities of Bonavista Bay. Legends recount that on one raid, he captured 9 vessels, 100 guns and canons, and 500 men. Although he was feared, he was welcomed by some because he sold stolen goods more cheaply than could be obtained elsewhere. What was the tragic end of this ruthless rogue? Not what you would expect! — He sailed peacefully to France, bought a castle, married a princess, and lived a very happy luxurious life!

Georgian Bay Islands National Park

Ontario

The scenery of these legendary islands has been immortalized on the canvases of the Canadian, Group of Seven, Artists. Their paintings have preserved for eternity the wind-swept trees, bared pink rock, jagged coastlines and transparent blue waters.

The reality is also protected, for generations to experience the myths and secrets of this land first hand. The islands that comprise the park have varied backgrounds. Those on the east side of Georgian Bay are adorned with 600 million year old quartz, granite, and gneiss. To the west, the islands have been shaped from limestone. The limestone pot shapes on Flowerpot Island have captured man's fantasy for years. Receding water levels and strong wave action eroded the limestone cliffs into the flowerpots or tapered columns at the water's edge. This island is steeped in mythical history. The flowerpots and quaint caves have been shrouded in ancient taboo. From under this cloak of taboo, blossom the delicate calypso orchids and the rare Alaska orchids. This abundant foral display adds to the fantasy of the island.

One of the much maligned creatures of myth and history finds an undisturbed refuge on Beausoleil Island. The endangered Massasauga rattlesnake, contrary to this reptile's reputation, timorously hides in the undisturbed swamp and marshy areas of this peaceful island.

There is a legend about the creation of Georgian Bay's Islands. Long ago, before the white man came, some Huron Braves, hunting off a great island in the north of Georgian Bay, heard a loud wailing in the woods. Any but Huron braves, would have fled in terror. But they followed the sound to its source and found a baby boy, the size of a full-grown man. They named him Kitchekawana, and believing him to be the son of the Great Spirit, Manitou, they called the large island Manitoulin Island — The Land of Manitou. Kitchekawana was adopted by the Hurons and brought to Huronia, on the southeastern shore of Georgian Bay, where he grew to an enormous size. Here, with his great hands, he scooped out the five bays of the nearby mainland, and hurled this mighty fistful of rock and soil to the north where it fell as the 30,000 islands.

Kitchekawana fell a bit short of the mark because there are actually 90,000 islands between Beausoleil Island in the southwestern corner of Georgina Bay and Manitoulin Island to the northwest. This constitutes the largest group of freshwater islands in the world. Seventy-seven of these island are being conserved in Georgian Bay Islands National Park so that generations upon generations can be amused by the legend and the reality of this whimsical area.

Cottage Cheese Bread

1¾ cups	whole-wheat flour	425 mL
¼ cup	wheat germ	50 mL
¼ cup	sugar	50 mL
4 tsp.	baking powder	20 mL
¼ tsp.	baking soda	1 mL
¼ tsp.	salt	1 mL
1 cup	cottage cheese	250 mL
¼ cup	vegetable oil	50 mL
2 tbsp.	molasses	30 mL
2	eggs	2
¾ cup	milk	175 mL
½ cup	raisins	125 mL

Combine dry ingredients and mix well. In a separate bowl combine cottage cheese, vegetable oil, molasses, eggs, and milk. Add raisins.

Add dry ingredients to liquid ingredients, and stir until moisture is absorbed. Pour batter into a greased 8" x 8" (20 cm x 20 cm) pan. Bake for 45-50 minutes at 350°F (180°C). Cut into squares and serve.

Kathie Anderson
Winnipeg, Man.

Riding Mountain
National Park

Jenny's Beer Bread

2½ cups	whole-wheat flour	625 mL
2 tsp.	baking powder	10 mL
1 tsp.	salt	5 mL
¼ tsp.	baking soda	1 mL
2 tsp.	sugar	10 mL
12 oz.	bottle beer (local brand)	341 mL
1 tbsp.	honey or molasses	15 mL
1 tbsp.	sesame seeds	15 mL

Combine flour, baking powder, salt, baking soda, and sugar. Add beer and mix well. Pour into a greased 8½" x 4½" (20 cm x 10 cm) loaf pan. Spoon honey or molasses down the centre and sprinkle sesame seeds on top. Bake for 1 hour at 350°F (180°C). Makes 1 loaf.

Jenny Feick
Glovertown, Nfld.

Terra Nova
National Park

Delicious served warm with butter and honey!

Eclectic Pancakes

1 cup	flour*	250 mL
1 tsp.	baking powder	5 mL
¼ cup	rolled oats	50 mL
¼ tsp.	cinnamon	1 mL
1	egg	1
1⅓ cups	milk	325 mL
1½ tsp.	melted butter	7 mL

Combine flour, baking powder, oats, and cinnamon in a large bowl.

In a separate bowl, beat egg lightly. Add milk and melted butter.

Add liquid ingredients slowly to dry ingredients, stirring until batter is mixed. The batter should flow thickly off a spoon. If it is too thick, add more milk; if it is too thin, add more flour.

You may wish to add some raisins, blueberries, apple, or banana slices or a tablespoon of cocoa for extra taste. Experiment! Pour pancake-sized portions onto a hot, lightly greased frying pan. Cook for about 2 minutes on each side or until lightly browned. Keep pancakes in a warm oven until you are ready to serve them.

Serve with warm maple syrup, yogurt, butter, nuts and/or raisins. Makes 8 medium pancakes.

*The flour can be all-purpose, whole-wheat, rye, triticale, buckwheat, or any combination of the above.

Ken Walker
Jasper, Alta.

Jasper
National Park

Favourite Pancakes

1	egg	1
1 cup	buttermilk	250 mL
2 tbsp.	melted shortening	30 mL
1 cup	flour	250 mL
1 tbsp.	sugar	15 mL
1 tsp.	baking powder	5 mL
½ tsp.	baking soda	2 mL
½ tsp.	salt	2 mL

Beat egg, add buttermilk and melted shortening. Sift dry ingredients and combine with liquid ingredients, stir until batter is fairly smooth. Drop by ¼ cupfuls (50 mL) onto hot, oiled griddle. Cook until pancakes are full of bubbles and underside is brown. Flip to cook other side. Makes 8 pancakes.

Ethel Lisowski
Brandon, Man.

Riding Mountain
National Park

Partridgeberry Muffins
(Mountain Cranberry)

1	egg	1
1 cup	milk	250 mL
¼ cup	vegetable oil	50 mL
2 cups	flour	500 mL
3 tsp.	baking powder	15 mL
⅛ tsp.	salt	0.5 mL
¼ cup	sugar	50 mL
¾-1 cup	partridgeberries	175-250 mL

In a small mixing bowl, beat egg. Add milk and vegetable oil and mix well. Set aside.

In a large mixing bowl, combine flour, baking powder, salt, and sugar. Make a well in the center. Pour liquid ingredients into dry ingredients, mixing quickly and lightly until flour is moistened. Do not beat — batter should be lumpy.

Fold in the berries with the last few strokes of mixing. Spoon into greased muffin tins and bake for approximately 25 minutes at 400°F (200°C). Makes 1 dozen medium muffins.

Chilomena Blackmore
Glovertown, Nfld.

Terra Nova
National Park

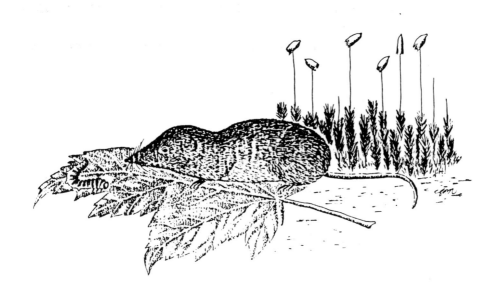

Point Pelee National Park

Ontario

Amidst the bustle of a densely populated region lies a rare, fragile jewel — Point Pelee National Park. It is too small and delicate to withstand heavy traffic, so there are no individual campsites and automobiles give way to pollution-free, trackless trains.

Since this is Canada's most southerly mainland point, the area nurtures many species of plant and animal life which are found only in southern climates. Spring first adorns Point Pelee with fragrant, vibrant summer flowers and only after decorating this delicate garden, does it move on to the rest of Canada.

One of the precious offerings of Point Pelee National Park is the preponderance of birds. This tiny refuge provides a nesting place for a vast variety of birds as they follow their migration routes. More than 100 species nest on this tranquil peninsula. The myriad of precious birds that cluster on this haven encourages many diligent birdwatchers to try for a "century day" when they sight 100 species in one day.

Explorers treasured the night's rest that enveloped them on this wilderness gem. In 1670, the missionary Fathers Dollier and Galenée encamped on this point. General Brock and his expeditionary force renewed their energy here in 1812 before their successful attack on Detroit.

One of the customs of the area is "smelting". In April, thousands join together on the beaches in comraderie and companionship. With their nets and hip-waders, they frantically chase the tiny fish, glittering like diamonds in the moonlight. Peals of laughters and excitement echo across the twilight depths as the merry chase continues!

For many, Point Pelee National Park is a treasurer trove of memories and exuberant beauty.

Yogurt Blueberry Bran Muffins

2 cups	plain yogurt	500 mL
2 tsp.	baking soda	10 mL
1½ cups	brown sugar	375 mL
2	eggs	2
1 cup	vegetable oil	250 mL
2 cups	bran	500 mL
2 tsp.	vanilla	10 mL
2 cups	flour	500 mL
4 tsp.	baking powder	20 mL
½ tsp.	salt	2 mL
1 cup	unsweetened blueberries	250 mL

Combine yogurt and baking soda. Set aside.

In a large mixing bowl, cream sugar and eggs. Add vegetable oil, bran, and vanilla and mix well.

Sift together the flour, baking powder, and salt. Add dry ingredients to the sugar mixture, alternating with the yogurt. Add blueberries and stir until evenly distributed.

Spoon into well-greased muffin tins, and bake for 35-40 minutes at 350°F (180°C). Makes about 1½ dozen muffins.

Beverly Rutherford
Field, B.C.

Yoho
National park

See photograph page 16.

DESSERTS

&

SWEETS

Bailey's Charlotte Renaissance

Jasper Park Lodge

3 cups	milk	750 mL
8	egg yolks	8
1¼ cups	sugar	300 mL
3½ tbsp.	unflavoured gelatin	25 g
2-3 drops	vanilla extract	2-3 drops
3 cups	whipping cream	750 mL
4	apples	4
1¼ cups	white wine	300 mL
1	cinnamon stick	1
1¼ cups	Bailey's Irish Cream Liqueur	300 mL
½ cup	whipping cream, whipped strawberries, or other fresh fruit	125 mL
24	ladyfingers	24
8 oz.	semisweet chocolate, melted	250 g

Combine milk, egg yolks, sugar, gelatin and vanilla extract in a saucepan. Cook 7-10 minutes over medium heat, until thick. Do not allow it to come to a boil. Remove from heat, and cool. (Either place the pan on a bed of crushed ice, or place in the refrigerator for approximately ½ hour.) Whip the cream. Fold whipped cream into the custard mixture. Divide custard into 2 portions.

Peel the apples, and cut into cubes. Set aside. Combine wine and cinnamon stick in a saucepan and bring to a boil. Remove cinnamon stick. Add the cubed apples, and continue to boil for 4 minutes. Drain off the liquid, and cool the apple pieces. Fold the apples into the first half of the creamed recipe. Pour the apple mixture into a 10" spring form pan or a cake pan, if you don't have a springform pan. Refrigerate until set.

Add the Bailey's Irish Cream to the second half of the custard. Mix well and place on top of the first layer. Refrigerate until top layer is set.

Remove the outer ring of the springform pan. Garnish the cake with whipped cream, strawberries, kiwi or other fresh fruit and ladyfingers dripped in melted chocolate. Serves 12.

Jasper Park Lodge
Jasper, Alta.

Jasper
National Park

The chefs at the Jasper Park Lodge concocted this delightful treat specifically for the National Parks Centennial. It is their hope that it will appeal to a great many hostesses who are looking for a new dessert!

Note: If you serve the ladyfingers beside each piece, 24 fingers are plenty. If you wish to put ladyfingers around the cake, you will need 2 packages of ladyfingers.

See photograph on cover.

Strawberry Dessert

14 oz.	pkg. graham wafers, crushed	400 g
½ cup	melted butter	125 mL
¼ cup	sugar	50 mL
2 - 15 oz.	pkg. frozen strawberries	2 - 425 g
1 tbsp.	lemon juice	15 mL
3 tbsp.	corn starch	45 mL
8 oz.	small package marshmallows	250 g
½ cup	milk	125 mL
1 cup	whipping cream	250 mL

Combine graham wafer crumbs, melted butter, and sugar. Reserve ¾ cup for the topping. Press the remaining crumbs into the bottom of an 8" x 12" (20 cm x 30 cm) pan.

Thaw frozen strawberries and drain, save the liquid. Combine the juice from the strawberries, lemon juice, and corn starch. Cook over medium heat for 5 minutes or until thick. Cool and combine with the strawberries.

In a double boiler, combine marshmallows and milk. Cook until marshmallows are melted. Cool. Whip the cream and fold into the cooled marshmallow mixture.

Pour ½ of the marshmallow mixture on the crumb crust. Spread the strawberry mixture on top and then add the remaining marshmallow mixture. Top with reserved crumbs. Refrigerate for 24 hours. Serves 8-10.

Helen Singleton
Winnipeg, Man.

Riding Mountain
National Park

Corporal Singleton was an R.C.M.P. officer, who was stationed at Riding Mountain National Park from 1954-1956. In this beautiful setting that the family called "home", Herb continued the R.C.M.P. tradition of establishing law and order. His task was probably more peaceful than some of his forbearers!

It was, in fact, violence in the Cypress Hills in 1873 that encouraged recruitment of the North West Mounted Police, the predecessor to the Royal Canadian Mounted Police. A police fort was established at Fort Walsh in 1875 and a district headquarters was organized at Battleford in 1876. Their purposes were to suppress the whiskey trade, establish contact with the Indians and bring law, order, and justice to the west.

The North West Mounted Police played a significant roll in the development of Western Canada.

This contribution is graphically depicted at Fort Walsh National Historic Park and Battleford National Historic Park.

Frosted Strawberry Squares

1 cup	flour	250 mL
¼ cup	brown sugar	50mL
½-¾ cup	chopped walnuts	125-175 mL
½ cup	melted butter	125 mL
2	egg whites	2
1 cup	sugar	250 mL
15 oz.	pkg. frozen strawberries, partially thawed	425 g
2 tbsp.	lemon juice	30 mL
1 cup	whipping cream	250 mL

Combine flour, brown sugar, chopped walnuts, and melted butter. Spread on a cookie sheet and bake for 20 minutes at 350°F (180°C), stirring often. Spread ⅔ of the crumbs in the bottom of a 13" x 9" (4 L) pan.

Combine egg whites, sugar, strawberries, and lemon juice in a large bowl. Beat with an electric Mixmaster for 10 minutes or until stiff peaks form.

Whip cream and fold into the strawberry mixture. Spoon this over the crumb crust and top with remaining crumbs. Freeze overnight. Remove from the freezer about ½ hour before serving. Serves 10.

This can be made in advance and frozen for about 2 weeks.

Mrs. Davidson
Winnipeg, Man.

Riding Mountain
National Park

See photograph page 128.

Clear Lake Surprise

19 oz.	can crushed pineapple, drained	540 mL
10 oz.	can mandarins, drained	284 mL
16 oz.	Cool Whip	500 g
3 oz.	pkg. peach Jell-o	85 g
½-1 cup	chopped nuts	125-250 mL
16 oz.	creamed cottage cheese	500 g

Combine all the ingredients and mix well. (Do not add water to the Jell-o powder — just add it as is.) Chill several hours. Serves 10.

Shiela Murphy
Winnipeg, Man.

Riding Mountain
National Park

St. Lawrence Islands National Park

Ontario

Before there was time and long before white men visited the St. Lawrence, petals of heavenly flowers fell to earth and were scattered on the mighty river-creating the Manitouana — "The Garden of the Great Spirit". Today part of this garden has become Canada's smallest national park — St. Lawrence Islands.

These islands are one of the oldest national parks in the country. In some respects, its claims go back further than Banff, our first official national park. By 1877, the Brockville Recorder and Times was calling a number of these islands a national park and the federal government appointed local fisheries officers as "Island Guardians." However, it was not until 1904 that the islands received official park status.

The first component of this profuse garden was the tiny lichen that clung precariously to the Precambrian granite. These first colonizers, proliferated and gradually broke off bits of rock. This rock mingled with the decaying lichen to become rich new soil. Gradually, a moss blanket covered the area and this nurtured the grasses, shrubs, and finally the canopy of deep emerald forests. This process still continues and can be seen in many places as the fragile lichen struggles for a foothold on the barren rock.

Some gardens are threatened by snakes. These island gardens, however, shelter the endangered Black Rat Snake as one of its most precious resources. This non-poisonous snake is the largest found in Canada.

Throughout the ages, man has admired the luxuriant beauty of these islands. Many passed by the Thousand Island in search of adventure and lured by promises, but none settled here until the 18th century, when the United Empire Loyalists began tilling the rocky soil. Soon mills, an iron works, a glass factory, and other industry sprang up in the area. During the war of 1912, these settlers found themselves on the most vital water route in the country. The river teamed with activity, as life-saving supplies, ammunition, and guns were shipped to Upper Canada. Peace returned to the garden and palatial homes and castles adorned their attractive shores. Over the years, the St. Lawrence Islands became transformed into a haven of leisure and recreational activity.

In the midst of this 20th century luxury, the essential character of the islands is little changed. Peace, in a profound sense, can be experienced in the idyllic "Garden of the Great Spirit" — the St. Lawrence Islands.

Peach Kuchen

2 cups	flour	500 mL
½ tsp.	salt	2 mL
½ cup	butter	125 mL
¼ tsp.	baking powder	1 mL
2 tbsp.	sugar	30 mL
4 cups	peaches, sliced	1 L
¾ cup	sugar	175 mL
1 tsp.	cinnamon	5 mL
2	egg yolks	2
1 cup	sour cream	250 mL
¼ tsp.	cinnamon	1 mL
2 tbsp.	sugar	30 mL

Combine flour, salt, butter, baking powder and sugar. Reserve ¼ cup (50 mL) for topping. Pat the remaining mixture into the bottom of an 8" x 8" (20 cm x 20 cm) pan. Lay sliced peaches on top.

Combine sugar, cinnamon, and reserved flour mixture. Sprinkle over peaches. Bake for 15 minutes at 400°F (200°C).

Combine egg yolks and sour cream, beat well. Pour over partially baked kuchen. Sprinkle with cinnamon and sugar. Return to the oven and bake 30 minutes. Serve hot or cold. Serves 6-8.

Norma Ferguson
Winnipeg, Man.

Riding Mountain
National Park

Wild Rice Fancy Dessert

½ cup	wild rice	125 mL
½ cup	brown sugar	125 mL
½ cup	nuts, chopped	125 mL
½ cup	dates, chopped	125 mL
½ cup	candied or maraschino cherries, choped	125 mL
1 cup	whipping cream	250 mL
1-2 tbsp.	icing sugar	15-30 mL
	amaretto to taste (optional)	

Cook wild rice according to package instructions. Drain and cool.

Combine brown sugar, nuts, dates, cherries and add to the rice. Chill for 2-3 hours.

Whip the cream. Add icing sugar and amaretto, if desired. Serve the dessert topped with whipped cream. This recipe is great for really putting on the dog!

Duane West
Alma, N.B.

Fundy
National Park

La Mauricie National Park

Québec

La Mauricie National Park is nestled in the knobbly, antiquated Laurentians. Reaching back to the beginnings of time, these grandmother mountains have a grace and wisdom that enriches with age. This range is over 950 million years old. It is ten times older than the Rockies. The ancient contours of these mountains are composed of metamorphic rock. Millions of years of erosion and glaciation have mellowed their exteriors and gentled their temperaments.

This nurturing land harboured the Attikamek Indians for 5,000 years. These nomadic people sought refuge in the fertile forests, travelling the meandering rivers in search of game, berries and roots. In the summer, the gathered at what is now Trois Riviéres. This was a time of socializing and bartering with the Iroquois. These Attikameks greeted the French settlers with friendship and probably introduced them to the joys of maple sugar!

At the beginning of the century, La Mauricie was logged extensively. Now, a timber slide, a dam, the ruins of a saw mill and memories are all that remain of this era. The park's first logger — the beaver — now has sole logging rights to the region. He triumphantly transforms the landscape, whimsically drying up some lakes and creating others.

La Mauricie National Park characterizes a beauty, improved with age, an elegance refined with experience. Her charm and grandeur invite you to share the secrets of time.

Saskatchewan Snowballs

½ cup	butter	125 mL
1 cup	sugar	250 mL
2	egg yolks, beaten	2
1 cup	crushed pineapple, drained	250 mL
1 cup	walnuts, finely chopped	250 mL
2	egg whites	2
7 oz.	pkg. vanilla wafers	200 g
2 cups	whipping cream	500 mL
	coconut	

Cream butter and sugar. Add beaten egg yolks, pineapple, and walnuts.

Beat the egg whites until stiff and fold them into the pineapple mixture.

Spread 1 vanilla wafer with this mixture. The filling should be about ½" (1.3 cm) thick. Place another wafer on top and spread ½" (1.3 cm) filling on top. Top with another wafer. Do not frost the top. Continue to make the rest of the snowballs in the same manner. Each snowball should have 3 wafers. Place them on a cookie sheet and refrigerate for 24 hours.

Two hours before serving time, whip the cream. Cover each snowball with whipped cream and sprinkle with coconut. Keep refrigerated. Makes 20.

Once the snowballs have been frosted, they can be kept frozen for 2-3 weeks. They can be decorated with candied fruit for Christmas, chocolate for Easter, or with candles for birthdays.

M. Brunsoman
Fountain Hills, Arizona

Riding Mountain
National Park

The Brunsomans travelled up from Bismark, North Dakota for 20 years to spend their summer at Clear Lake. When they bought their summer home in 1948, they had to cut out 98 trees. The Brunsomans were avid golfers and they cut off some golf clubs so that their sons could enjoy the lovely golf course while they were young.

Apple Crisp

6	large apples, peeled and sliced	6
½ cup	orange juice	125 mL
½ cup	sugar	125 mL
¾ cup	flour	175 mL
½ cup	light brown sugar	125 mL
½ tsp.	cinnamon	2 mL
¼ tsp.	salt	1 mL
6 tbsp.	butter	90 mL

Arrange apples in a greased 9″ x 9″ (23 cm x 23 cm) baking dish. Pour the orange juice over top.

Combine the remaining ingredients to make a crumbly mixture. Spread over the apple slices. Bake for 45-50 minutes at 350°F (180°C).

Tony Barnstead
Winnipeg, Man.

Riding Mountain
National Park

This is a simple, delicious dessert! If you want to dress it up a bit, serve with cream or whipped cream.

Yukon Blueberry Syrup

2 cups	blueberries	500 mL
1 cup	sugar	250 mL
½ cup	water	125 mL

Combine all the ingredients in a saucepan. Boil until the berries are soft and then put them through a sieve. Seal in pint jars. Use over hot-cakes, waffles or biscuits. Makes about 2 cups (500 mL).

Kluane
National Park Reserve

Apple Pan Dowdy

1 cup	flour	250 mL
1 tbsp.	baking powder	15 mL
1 tsp.	sugar	5 mL
¼ tsp.	salt	1 ml
2 tbsp.	butter	30 mL
½ cup	milk	125 mL
2 cups	apples, peeled, finely chopped or grated	500 mL
½ tsp.	nutmeg	2 mL
1-2 tbsp.	butter, cut into bits	15-30 mL
1 cup	brown sugar	250 mL
⅛ tsp.	salt	0.5 mL
1 tbsp.	flour	15 mL
1 cup	boiling water	250 mL
2 tbsp.	butter	30 mL

Combine flour, baking powder, sugar, and salt. Cut in butter. Add milk and stir until a dough forms. Knead 10-12 times on a floured board.

Roll dough into a thin rectangle. Spread with grated apples. Sprinkle with nutmeg and bits of butter. Roll up like a jelly roll. Cut into 2" (5 cm) slices and place them on a greased 8" x 8" (20 cm x 20 cm) baking dish.

Combine brown sugar, salt, flour, boiling water, and butter. Stir until smooth. Pour over biscuits. Bake for 15-20 minutes at 450°F (230°C) or until brown. Serves 4-6.

Bernie McKenzie
Rivers, Man.

Riding Mountain
National Park

This is a disaster for a sweet tooth!

The McKenzie log cabin is two years older than Riding Mountain National Park.

The 4th generation of McKenzies have come to love Clear Lake as much as their great-grandparents had hoped they would when they bought the cabin forty years ago.

Auyuittuq National Park Reserve

Northwest Territories

Auyuittuq, "the land that never melts" lives up to its Inuit name. It is an encounter in an elemental, unpredictable wilderness. This harsh unspoiled land is the only arctic park in the world. Its rugged features challenge and entice the hardy and adventurous.

It is, in fact, an adventure even getting to this park! The only access to Auyuittuq is by Inuit freighter canoe, by snowmobile, or on foot. Departures and arrivals of canoes or boats are hampered by the tides. Canoes can only arrive or depart from Pangnirtung within two hours either side of high tide. Water transportation is also limited by the life-threatening, frequently vengeful winds. In addition to this precarious access, transportation is further determined by break-up and freeze-up of the fjord. Each lasts for about two weeks from mid-June to mid-July and from mid-October to mid-November. The access from Broughton Island is not hampered by the tides and winds but usually doesn't open up until early August.

Once you have accomplished these challenges, the elusive grandeur of this solitary land beckons. You can meet it only with self-sufficiency expertise, and strength! There are many obstacles in this land of winter-darkness and summer-sunlight. The major force to be reckoned with is the capriciousness of nature with its gale-force winds, rock slides, and severe ice falls. The rugged splendour of the rolling, ice glaciers, precipitous fjords, and the intriguing arctic wildlife are rare treasured experiences.

Despite the formidable domain, it has been home for the Inuit for thousands of years. Archaeologists have unearthed stone tools of the Pre-Dorset and Dorset peoples (2,000 B.C.-1,300 A.D.) and have delicately revealed the stone-walled houses of the Thule culture. The Thules or "people of the seal" are the ancestors of the Inuit.

John Davis was the first European to explore the area and named the Cumberland Peninsula in 1585. Interest in the area was not sparked until 1840 when William Penny mentioned sighting whales. This observation aroused the curiosity of Scottish whalers and inspired them to establish a settlement. It was abandoned in 1925, but the iron vats used for boiling down the whale blubber still serve as a lonely reminder of human habitation.

Auyuittuq still offers a challenge that only a few accept, but those who forge into this isolated wilderness return with its mystery and beauty imbedded in their hearts!

Fireweed and Clover Honey

30	clover flowers	30
18	fireweed flowers	18
2½ cups	water	625 mL
10 cups	sugar	2.5 L
1 tsp.	powdered alum	5 mL

Wash the flowers. Boil flowers and water for 10 minutes. Let it steep to increase the flavour. Strain out the flowers. Add sugar and alum. Boil 10 minutes. Pour into sterilized jars.

Doris Papineau
Dezadeash Lake, Yukon

Kluane
National Park Reserve

West Coast Blackberry Jam

(With Low Sugar and No Artifical Pectin)

5 cups	blackberries	1.25 L
1 cup	sugar	250 mL
½ cup	lemon juice	125 mL
6-8 tsp.	arrowroot	30-40 mL

Crush berries slightly. Boil the berries and sugar for 5 minutes. Add the lemon juice and arrowroot and boil for 5 minutes more. Put into jars and seal. Makes about 5 cups (1250 mL).

This jam is thinner than most jams, but is delicious and ideal for those who wish to cut down on sugar. If you wish a sweeter jam, just add more sugar. The arrowroot used as a thickener gives the jam a clear bright colour. If you prefer a thicker jam, add more arrowroot.

Note: Raspberries may be used instead of blackberries.

Dorothy Arnet
Tofino, B.C.

Pacific Rim
National Park

Dorothy has worked at Pacific Rim since October 1980 as secretary to the Superintendent. She lives in Tofino, at the end of Highway No. 4 — next stop Japan! Her home overlooks Browning Passage — the harbour of Tofino. The village has a population of about 800 people and is one of the most picturesque fishing villages on the West Coast. Rarities such as salmon, crab, shrimp, scallops, and abalone are a regular item in the Arnet home, and in the summer, blackberries are so abundant that they make jars and jars of jam.

CAKES
&
PIES

Blackberry and Apple Cake

Banff Springs Hotel

FILLING

5½ cups	apples	650 g
½ tsp.	cornstarch	2 mL
1 tbsp.	lemon juice	15 mL
3¼ cups	blackberries	400 g
⅔ cups	sugar	160 g

Peel, core and slice the apples. Combine cornstarch and lemon juice. Stir until smooth. Combine all the ingredients and mix well. Spread over prepared crust.

DOUGH

1 cup	butter	200 g
1 cup	sugar	200 g
1	egg	1
1¾ cups	ground hazelnuts	200 g
⅛ tsp.	salt	0.5 mL
1 cup	white cake crumbs	100 g
1 cup	flour	200 g
1 tsp.	baking powder	5 mL

Cream butter and sugar together. Lightly beat the egg and add it to the creamed mixture. Mix in hazelnuts, salt, and cake crumbs. Combine flour and baking powder and fold it into the creamed mixture.

Roll the dough out to ¼" (1 cm). Line the bottom and sides of a lightly greased 9" (23 cm) round cake pan. You may have to piece the dough and pat it together.

Fill the crust with prepared filling. Cut any leftover dough into ½" (1.3 cm) strips. Arrange them on top of the filling in a decorative pattern. Bake for 45 minutes at 350°F (180°C). Serves 6-8.

M. Luthi
Banff Springs Hotel, Banff, Alta.

Banff
National Park

Poor prairie folk who don't have blackberries, can try strawberries or raspberries instead.

Mrs. Mac's Carrot Cake

Lake O'Hara Lodge

2 cups	flour	500 mL
1 tsp.	salt	5 mL
1 tsp.	baking soda	5 mL
2 tsp.	cinnamon	10 mL
1 tsp.	baking powder	5 mL
1½ cups	salad oil	375 mL
2 cups	sugar	500 mL
4	eggs	4
2 cups	carrots, very finely chopped	500 mL

Sift together flour, salt, baking soda, cinnamon, and baking powder.

In a separate bowl, combine salad oil and sugar. Mix well. Add the oil mixture to the dry ingredients. Add the eggs, 1 at a time, beating well after each addition. Add chopped carrots and mix well.

Pour batter into 2 greased 8" (20 cm) layer cake pans. Bake for 50-60 minutes at 350°F (180°C). Turn onto racks to cool. When cooled, fill and frost with nutty icing. Serves 10-12.

NUTTY ICING

¼ cup	margarine	50 mL
8 oz.	cream cheese	250 g
1 lb.	icing sugar	500 g
1 tsp.	vanilla	5 mL
1 cup	chopped pecans	250 mL

Beat margarine and cream cheese until light and fluffy. Add the icing sugar, vanilla, and pecans and beat well. Fill and frost carrot cake. Keep refrigerated.

Lake O'Hara Lodge
Banff, Alta.

Banff
National Park

One of the early explorers to the Lake O'Hara region was Colonel Robert O'Hara. O'Hara had a reputation as unpopular with his guides. He had an extremely short temper and a stern, regimented, military outlook. On one occasion, the irascible O'Hara reprimanded his guide, James Tabuteau for swearing. He insisted that the guide count to three when the urge overcame him. After making camp one evening, Tabuteau glimpsed a burning ember from the campfire as it landed on O'Hara's tent. O'Hara noticed the guide's expression but not the tent! He rigidly enforced his edict. The exasperated Tabuteau slowly counted to three and exploded. "Colonel, your goddam tent's on fire!"

Gateau du Miette (Crumb Cake)

2 cups	flour	500 mL
1 cup	sugar	250 mL
¾ cup	lard	175 mL
1	egg	1
1 cup	milk	250 mL
½ tsp.	baking soda	2 mL
2 tsp.	baking powder	10 mL
1 tsp.	cloves	5 mL
1 tsp.	cinnamon	5 mL
1 cup	raisins	250 mL

In a bowl, mix flour and sugar. Cut in lard until mixture is crumb-like. Reserve 1 cup (250 mL) for topping. Add remaining ingredients.

Stir until ingredients are moistened. Pour into a greased 8" x 8" (20 cm x 20 cm) cake pan. Spread the reserved crumb mixture on top of the cake. Bake for 45 minutes at 375°F (190°C). Makes 16 pieces.

Yves Bossé   *Kouchibouguac*
St. Louis de Kent, N.B.   *National Park*

The crumb topping makes an easy, fancy cake. It won't last long!

Gateau du Miette

2 tasses	de farine blanche	500 mL
¾ tasse	de sain doux	175 mL
1 tasse	de sucre blanc	250 mL
1	oeuf	1
1 tasse	de lait	250 mL
½ c.	à thé soda	2 mL
2 c.	à thé poudre a pate	10 mL
½ c.	à thé de sel	2 mL
1 c.	à thé clou de giroffle	5 mL
1 c.	à thé de cannelle	5 mL
1 tasse	de raisin	250 mL

Mélanger le farine blanche, le sain doux et le sucre blanche et garder une tasse pour mettre dessus le gâteau. Ajouter au reste de mélange.

Vider le mélange dans une casserole 8" x 8". Par dessus la pâte, saupoudrer le mélange que vous avez sauvez au début. Cuire à 375°F pour 45 minutes.

Yves Bossé   *Kouchibouguac*
At. Louis de Kent, N.B.   *National Park*

Forillon National Park

Québec

Forillon is a relationshp — a co-existence between the land, the sea, and man. This brave peninsula firmly maintains its position between the Gulf of St. Lawrence and the Bay of Gaspé.

This distinctive piece of land extended its hospitality to early fishermen on expeditions from France and Spain. They would preserve their catch by drying it in the security of the pebble-dotted beaches. The fish dried quickly in the arid summers. Because little salt was needed, the mild Gaspé cure became the most coveted dried cod in the world. Gradually, the fishermen and their families accepted the invitation of this welcoming land. They established their homes atop the gleaming cliff-tops to avoid the long journeys back to Europe between fishing seasons.

Sometimes the life of the fishermen was more precarious on shore than on the turbulent, relentless seas. Often, in Grand Grève, the poverty-stricken fishermen could not afford their essential fishing equipment. The enterprising merchants would lend them goods or money. However, the price of the loan was established only after the last haul was in.

Curiously, the income of the poor honest fishermen never exceeded the loans and they were always indebted to these crafty businessmen.

The relationship between man and this coastal environment still exists today as scuba divers enthusiastically explore the coastal shoreline discovering a wealth of arctic plant and animal species. Here in this inviting atmosphere, Forillon National Park continues the tradition of fostering harmony between the land, the sea, and man.

Vinatorta

PRUNE FILLING

1 lb.	prunes	500 g
	water	
1 tbsp.	cinnamon	15 mL
¾ cup	sugar	175 mL

Cover the prunes with water. Simmer for 30 minutes or until plump and tender. Drain the prunes. Reserve ½ cup (125 mL) of the liquid. Allow the prunes to cool and remove the pits.

Blend the prunes in a blender, or cut into small pieces with scissors. Combine prunes, reserved liquid, cinnamon, and sugar in a saucepan. Simmer until the mixture is thick like jam. Cool.

Note: As a variation, you can use half prunes and half dates.

CAKE

1 cup	butter	250 mL
1½ cup	sugar	375 mL
2	eggs	2
3 tbsp.	cream	45 mL
1 tsp.	almond extract	5 mL
¼ tsp.	cardamon or cinnamon	1 mL
1 cup	flour	250 mL
3 cups	flour	750 mL
1 tsp.	baking powder	5 mL
⅛ tsp.	salt	0.5 mL
¼ cup	milk	50 mL

Cream butter thoroughly. Gradually add sugar, creaming well after each addition. Add the eggs 1 at a time, beating well after each egg. Add cream, almond extract, cardamom, and 1 cup flour. Beat well again.

Blend the remaining 3 cups flour with baking powder and salt. Add flour mixture to the batter alternately with the milk. Blend well. Refrigerate dough for easier handling.

Divide dough into 5 pieces. On a lightly floured board, roll out each piece until it is very thin. It should be about 8" (20 cm) in diameter. Take an 8' (20 cm) round pan and turn it upside down. Place the dough on the greased bottom. Trim the edges. Bake for 15-20 minutes at 350°F (180°C) or until delicately browned. Slide the cake gently onto a wire rack to cool. Repeat with the other layers. Bake as many layers at a time as you have pans and oven space for.

When all the layers are cool, spread 4 layers with prune filling. Stack the layers together, and place the fifth layer on top. Wrap the cake in plastic wrap and let it age for 3-7 days. Serves 14-18.

As you enjoy this recipe, you are sharing the treasured delight of the "Smorgasbord" that was held at Danvers Church. Many people holidaying at Riding Mountain National Park enjoyed this annual feast!

Cathy Furevick
Erickson, Man.

Riding Mountain
National Park

Similar recipe also contributed by:
Jacoslan Szlar
Lake Louise, Alta.

Banff
National Park

Apple Cake

1½ cups	vegetable oil	375 mL
2 cups	sugar	500 mL
3	eggs	3
3 cups	flour	750 mL
1 tsp.	salt	5 mL
1 tsp.	baking soda	5 mL
1 tsp.	vanilla	5 mL
1 cup	walnuts, chopped	250 mL
1 cup	raisins	250 mL
3 cups	Delicious apples, peeled, cored and thickly sliced	750 mL

In a mixing bowl, beat the oil and sugar together. Add the eggs and beat until creamy.

Sift the dry ingredients together and stir to blend. The batter will be very thick and dry. Turn into a well-greased and floured Bundt or angel cake pan. Bake for 1 hour and 15 minutes, or until done, at 350°F (180°C). Cool in the pan before turning out. Serve at room temperature with ice cream or whipped cream. Serves 10-12.

Eleanor Murray
Winnipeg, Man.

Riding Mountain
National Park

and her sister
Alison Rousset
Montreal, Que.

Riding Mountain
National Park

Beet Chocolate Cake

1½ cup	sugar	375 mL
3	eggs	3
1 cup	oil	250 mL
1½ cups	beets, raw, peeled and grated	375 mL
2	squares melted, unsweetened chocolate	2
1¾ cups	flour	424 mL
1½ tsp.	baking soda	7 mL
¼ tsp.	salt	1 mL
¼ tsp.	vanilla	1 mL

Combine sugar, eggs, oil, beets, and melted chocolate. Mix well.

Sift flour, baking soda, and salt. Add to the beet mixture and mix well. Stir in vanilla. Pour batter into a greased 9" x 9" (23 cm x 23 cm) pan. Bake for 50 minutes at 350°F (180°C). Makes 16 pieces.

Karen Townsend
Albert, N.B.

Fundy
National Park

Blueberry Cake

¼ cup	butter or margarine	50 mL
1½ cup	sugar	375 mL
1	egg	1
1 tsp.	vanilla	5 mL
1 cup	sour cream	250 mL
1 tsp.	baking soda	5 mL
2 cups	flour	500 mL
2 cups	blueberries	500 mL
1 tsp.	cinnamon	5 mL
½ cup	brown sugar	125 mL

Cream butter and sugar.

Combine egg, vanilla, and sour cream.

Mix baking soda with the flour. Add the sour cream mixture to the butter/sugar mixture alternately with the flour. Mix well and add blueberries. Spread batter in a greased 9" x 9" (23 cm x 23 cm) pan.

Combine cinnamon and brown sugar. Sprinkle over cake. Bake for 35-45 minutes at 350° (180°C). Makes 16 pieces.

NOTE: Chopped rhubarb can be used instead of blueberries.

Doreen Langdon
Winnipeg, Man.

Riding Mountain
National Park

Kouchibouguac National Park

New Brunswick

Change and transformation characterize Kouchibouguac National Park. It is a dynamically changing ecosystem. The chain of barrier islands are moulded by a whimsical sea. The dunes, reefs, and lagoons shift with nature's artistic hand. The forceful storm-aroused waves wrench the sand, the land, and the sea bottom and toss it into ridges along the beach. The crests of the dunes are caressed and chiseled by wind. The major dunes North Kouchibouguac, South Kouchibouguac, and Richibucto have eluded permanent shape for 2,500 years. Their metamorphic designs creep gradually, ever-changing towards the magnetic shore.

These island ramparts shelter placid lagoons from the sometimes violent sea. In the lagoons, the searching salt water explores and mingles with the fresh water from the vital streams and rivers of the park. As a raging storm alters the island contours, it transforms the life of the lagoons, estuaries, and salt marshes.

As the coast is sculpted by the sea, the forests have been molded by man. The forests have been logged and burned continually during the past few centuries. The tall white pine became ship masts. Other trees were also used in ship building. The land was cleared as well for animal grazing and for crops. Now these areas are cautiously seeking their way back to their natural state.

The human history of Kouchibouguac presents a picture of change and diversity as well. The Mic Mac Indians first staked claim to the area and the park now bears the Mic Mac name Kouchibouguac, "River of the Long Tides." Early Acadians introduced their culture to the area. And the United Empire Loyalists brought their influence with them. Finally, the customs stabilized with a predominantly Acadian character. However, the legends, customs, foods, medicines, and music still intermingle. They all retain many similarities induced by the natural habitats in the region.

Kouchibouguac is an ever-present reminder of the elusive, constantly changing nature of the universe!

Summer Shower Flan

3	large eggs	3
⅓ cup	sugar	75 mL
2 tsp.	baking powder	10 mL
8 tbsp.	flour	120 mL
⅛ tsp.	salt	0.5 mL
2 tsp.	vanilla	10 mL
3½ oz.	pkg. lemon pie filling	113 g
½ cup	sugar	125 mL
¼ cup	water	50 mL
2	egg yolks	2
1 cup	hot water	250 mL
1 tbsp.	butter	15 mL
	assorted decorative fruits	
½ oz.	pkg. Oetkers transparent pie filling base (or ½ cup (125 mL) apple jelly)	15 g

Oil a 12" (30 cm) flan pan thoroughly. Make sure to oil each ridge.

Beat the eggs until foamy and light. Slowly add ⅓ cup (75 mL) sugar.

Combine baking powder, flour, and salt. Add this to the egg mixture and mix well. Add vanilla. Pour batter into the greased flan pan. Bake for 10-12 minutes at 325°F (160°C), or until lightly coloured. Don't let it get too brown.

Combine lemon pie filling with ½ cup (125 mL) sugar and ¼ cup (50 mL) water in a saucepan. Add the egg yolks and blend well. Gradually add hot water, and stir over medium heat until it comes to a boil and thickens. Stir in butter. Cool for 5 minutes.

Turn the cooled flan onto a fancy serving plate. Spread with lemon pie filling. Place strawberry halves, grape halves, mandarin orange segments, pineapple rings (or any other fruit) in a decorative pattern on top of the lemon pie filling. Place the fruit close together, so that it completely covers the pie filling.

Prepare the Oetker transparent pie filling base according to the package instructions. Pour over the fruit. Make sure that the fruit is completely covered.

If you wish to use apple jelly instead, melt the jelly in a saucepan. Cool for 5 minutes and then pour over the fruit, covering it completely. Serves 8-10.

NOTE: for a 10" flan use:

2	eggs	2
¼ cup	sugar	50 mL
1½ tsp.	baking powder	7 mL
6 tbsp.	flour	90 mL
1½ tsp.	vanilla	7 mL

Prepare filling and fruit as above.

Marj Stewart
Winnipeg, Man.

Riding Mountain
National Park

Over the years we have always looked for an excuse to give someone a shower. Clear Lake has provided the perfect setting. On these occasions, there is nothing more festive than a fresh fruit flan!

See photograph page 48.

Mock Cherry Pie

4 tbsp	flour	60 mL
1½ cups	sugar	375 mL
½ tsp.	salt	2 mL
1 cup	water	500 mL
3 cups	low bush cranberries, washed	750 mL
1 cup	raisins, scalded	250 mL
½ tsp.	almond extract	2 mL
	pastry for a 2 crust pie	

Combine flour, sugar, and salt in a saucepan. Add water and bring slowly to a boil, stirring constantly. Add the cranberries and raisins. Bring back to a boil and simmer 5 minutes, stirring constantly. Remove from heat. Add almond extract and cool.

Pour filling into a prepared pie crust. Cover with top crust. Bake for 15 minutes at 425°F (220°C). Turn down the heat to 375°F (190°C) and bake for another 30 minutes or until crust is lightly browned. Serves 6-8.

This is an unusual way to use cranberries, and is a nice change from cranberry sauce. The cranberry/raisin combination makes a tangy pie filling that tastes amazingly like cherries. It's fabulous with ice cream.

Merna Forster
Jasper, Alta.

Jasper
National Park

Cranberry Pie

Chateau Lake Louise

PASTRY

2 cups	flour	500 mL
1 tsp.	salt	5 mL
½ cup	cold butter	125 mL
4 tbsp.	water, with 2 ice cubes in it	60 mL
1 tsp.	vinegar	5 mL

Combine flour and salt. Cut in the butter until pea-sized balls are formed.

Combine the ice water and the vinegar. Remove ice cubes, and pour liquid ingredients into flour mixture. Mix until dough forms a ball in the centre of the bowl. Avoid using your hands to mix the dough. Wrap dough in plastic wrap and chill until you are ready to use it.

FILLING

2 cups	cranberries (fresh or frozen)	500 mL
¼ cup	water	50 mL
1 cup	sugar	250 mL
1 cup	raisins	250 mL

Wash and pick over the cranberries. Cook them in a little water until the cranberries are tender. Watch them carefully so they do not burn. Add sugar and raisins and mix well.

Pour filling into a 9" (23 cm) uncooked pastry shell. Use remaining dough to form a lattice top. Bake for 10 minutes at 425°F (220°C). Reduce heat to 350°F (180°C) and bake for 30 minutes. Serves 6-8.

Jaroslav Nydr, Executive Chef
Chateau Lake Louise, Lake Louise, Alta.

Banff
National Park

Fundy National Park

New Brunswick

Fundy National Park is an experience in the ebb and flow of existence. One cannot help but give way to the sway of the ever-present tides as the ocean expanse squeezes itself into the long, funnel-shaped bay. The extreme tides are pulled by two forces. The resonance of the water in the nearly enclosed bay sloshes back and forth down its length about every 13 hours. This, combined with the gravitational pull of the moon which occurs roughly simultaneously, reinforces tidal extremes. As the pulsating waters retreat, they unveil a fantasy world of periwinkles, limpets, barnacles, sea anenomes, and sand hoppers.

This oscillation extends to the forested areas of the parks as well. They are presently recovering from a century of careless logging which occured before the park was established in 1948. With park protection, the original balsam, alder, fir and, white and red spruce are returning to the area. Despite conservation efforts, the forests are still vulnerable. A large expanse of the forest has been attacked by budworms. This deceased forest is giving way to a natural regeneration of mixed species which are replacing the budworm-killed stands.

The ebb and flow of human activity has also influenced the Fundy area. The original inhabitants were the Archaic and the Mic Mac Indians who followed their food supply through the land. In the 16th century French and Portuguese fishermen visited the region. The Portuguese christened the bay Rio Fondu, meaning "deep river". The present name Fundy is an adaptation of this. In 1604, Samuel de Champlain claimed the bay as a French colony of Acadia. It later became Nova Scotia under British rule. In 1784, New Brunswick separated from Nova Scotia claiming the Bay of Fundy as its prize.

The area was settled by potato-famine Irish and post-Loyalist Americans. Lumbering became an important industry which generated shipping activity. Three-masted schooners, barques and barquentines gaily adorned the bay as they loaded lumber. Farmers labouriously tilled the stony glacial soil. Their meagre living was supplemented by lumbering, fishing, and hunting. As the lumbering subsided, settlements and farms were abondoned. When the park was established, several families were moved out completing this slow process of depopulation. Now this living outdoor museum portrays the rhythm and drama of the bold, irregular coastline.

Sour Cream Raisin Pie

Alternative in Fine Dining Restaurant

1	pastry shell, unbaked	1
2	eggs	2
¾ cup	sugar	175 mL
½ tsp.	cinnamon	2 mL
⅛ tsp.	cloves	0.5 mL
2 cups	sour cream	500 mL
1 cup	raisins	250 mL
3 tbsp.	flour	45 mL

Combine eggs, sugar, cinnamon, cloves, and sour cream.

Dust raisins with the flour and fold into sour cream mixture. Pour into the pie shell and bake for 35 minutes at 375°F (190°C). Serves 6-8.

This is the specialty dessert of the "Alternative in Fine Dining Restaurant", Riding Mountain National Park.

Ruth Aikens
Wasagaming, Man.

Riding Mountain
National Park

Rum Cream Pie

2 cups	graham wafer crumbs	500 mL
¼ tsp.	cinnamon	1 mL
½ cup	melted butter	125 mL
6	egg yolks	6
1 cup	sugar	250 mL
1 tbsp.	unflavoured gelatin	30 mL
½ cup	cold water	125 mL
2 cups	whipping cream	500 mL
½ cup	rum	125 mL
1 square	semisweet chocolate	1 square

Combine graham wafer crumbs and cinnamon. Add melted butter, mix well. Pat into a pie plate, bake for about 8 minutes at 375°F (190°C). Cool.

Beat egg yolks. Add sugar gradually and beat until thick and pale in colour.

Combine gelatin and cold water in the top of a double boiler. Heat until gelatin is dissolved. Add about 15 mL of the hot gelatin mixture to the egg yolk mixture. Stir well. Gradually add the remaining hot gelatin liquid to the egg yolk mixture, stirring constantly. Whip cream. Fold cream and rum into the filling. Pour into cooled pie shell. Refrigerate overnight. Just before serving, sprinkle with grated chocolate.

Jan Hlynsky
Vancouver, B.C.

Riding Mountain
National Park

COOKIES & SQUARES

Cream Wafers

1 cup	butter	250 mL
2 cups	flour	500 mL
⅓ cup	whipping cream	75 mL
	sugar	

Combine butter and flour. Mix together by hand. Add whipping cream and form batter into a ball. Place in the refrigerator to chill.

Roll the dough out thinly, and cut with a cookie cutter. Pat each side of the cookie in sugar. Place cookies on an ungreased cookie sheet. Prick with a fork.

Bake 7-9 minutes at 375°F (190°C), until light gold. Make about 1 cup (250 mL) of your favourite butter icing. Spread the top of one cookie with a little icing and put another cookie on top. Continue in this manner until you have used all the cookies. Makes about 2½ to 3 dozen.

Note: For special occasions, you can colour the icing appropriate colours.

Vivian Bicknell
Brandon, Man.

Riding Mountain
National Park

See photograph page 128.

Pecan Crispies

½ cup	butter or margarine	125 mL
6 tbsp.	white sugar	90 mL
6 tbsp.	brown sugar	90 mL
1	egg	1
½ tsp.	vanilla	2 mL
1¼ cups	flour, sifted	300 mL
1 tsp.	baking powder	5 mL
¼ tsp.	baking soda	1 mL
¼ tsp.	salt	1 mL
1 cup	pecans, chopped	250 mL

Cream butter and sugars. Add egg and vanilla, beat well.

Combine flour, baking powder, baking soda, and salt. Add to the creamed mixture and mix well. Add pecans. Drop from a teaspoon onto ungreased cookie sheets. Bake for about 10 minutes at 350°F (180°C). Cool cookies slightly before removing from the pan. Makes about 2½ dozen.

Roxie Ennes
Onanole, Man.

Riding Mountain
National Park

Prince Edward Island National Park

Prince Edward Island

Prince Edward Island National Park is sand — sand fantasy, wrinkling your bare foot, tugging and teasing as you step along; sand illusion — riffling and glimmering along the ocean dampened beach. In fact, the whole island is an accumulation of sand and mud deposited in a large ocean basin. Over time, the assemblage formed sandstone. The beaches of the park were created as the sandstone disintegrated into soft grains of sand. Some of the sand is carried offshore by mischievious waves and currents and modeled in merriment into sand bars and barrier islands. The violent turbulence of the sea edges the barrier islands forward, depositing a vastness of shimmering sand on the beaches. The beach sand is herded further onshore by playful winds and trapped firmly by the long, web-roots of the marram grass. Thus, the dunes are born. The combination of sand and dunes evokes ecstatic memories of youth.

Childhood fantasies are also tantalized by Green Gables House in Cavendish. You can visit the charming farmhouse where "Anne of Green Gables" lived or traced her footsteps down Lover's Lane, through Balsam Hollow and around the Lake of Shining Waters!

Another place, steeped in memory and tradition, is Dalvay-by-the-Sea. It was built as the summer residence of Alexander MacDonald in 1896. And it resembles his ancestral home in Scotland. This grand manor was eventually acquired by the park and now serves as a hotel and dining room.

Old dikes and bases of old earthen fences serve as a reminder of earlier settlers. Europeans first arrived in the area in 1770 and depended on the land and the sea for their living. For generations, people fished from these shores. More recently, the harvesting of Irish moss has developed into a thriving industry. Another important activity, in times gone by, was the trading of illicit rum during Prohibition. If you look carefully, you can still see the secretive remains of the small pits where enterprising residents stashed the precious rum barrels.

From the echoes of the past, Prince Edward Island National Park stands as a chronicle and a tribute to sand, fantasy, and memory.

Jumbo Raisin Cookies

2 cups	raisins	500 mL
1 cup	water	250 mL
1 cup	margarine	250 mL
2 cups	sugar	500 mL
3	eggs	3
1 tsp.	vanilla	5 mL
4 cups	flour	1 L
1 tsp.	baking soda	5 mL
1 tsp.	baking powder	5 mL
½ tsp.	salt	2 mL
2 tsp.	mixed spices of your choice (cinnamon, nutmeg, etc.)	10 mL

Combine raisins and water in a saucepan. Boil for 5 minutes and allow them to cool.

Cream margarine, sugar, and eggs. Add vanilla.

Sift together flour, baking soda, baking powder, salt, and spices.

Add cooled raisins and water to the creamed mixture. Add dry ingredients and mix well. Drop from a dessert spoon onto greased cookie sheets. Bake for 10-12 minutes at 400°F (200°C), until lightly brown. Makes about 3 dozen big yummy cookies that won't last long.

Gladys Meldrum
Wasagaming, Man.

Riding Mountain
National Park

Meldrum's store is a hub of activity at Clear Lake. People often stop for a chat while they are picking up the mail. Meldrum's has been in business since 1960, but four generations of the Meldrum family have enjoyed summers in Riding Mountain National Park since 1934.

Super Nutrition Cookies

1 cup	margarine	250 mL
1 cup	dark brown sugar (Demerara)	250 mL
½ cup	honey	125 mL
1 tsp.	vanilla	5 mL
2	eggs, beaten	2
1¾ cup	whole-wheat flour	425 mL
1 tsp.	baking soda	5 mL
1 tsp.	salt	5 mL
1 cup	oatmeal	250 mL
½ cup	wheat germ	125 mL
12 oz.	chocolate chips	340 g
	or	
2 cups	raisins	500 mL
	or	
1 cup	raisins and	250 mL
1 cup	chocolate chips	250 mL

Cream margarine, sugar, and honey. Add vanilla and eggs.

Combine flour, baking soda and salt. Mix well. Add to the creamed mixture. Add remaining ingredients.

Drop the batter from a teaspoon onto a greased cookie sheet. Bake for 8-10 minutes at 350°F (180°C). Makes about 5 dozen.

Stella MacLean
Alma, N.B.

Fundy
National Park

See photograph page 128.

Unbaked Caramel Cookies

2 cups	sugar	500 mL
¾ cup	butter or margarine	175 mL
⅔ cup	evaporated milk	150 mL
4 oz.	package butterscotch instant pudding	115 g
3½ cups	quick-cooking rolled oats	875 mL

In a large saucepan, combine the sugar, butter, and evaporated milk. Bring the mixture to a boil, stirring frequently.

Remove from heat and add the pudding and rolled oats. Mix together thoroughly. Cool 15 minutes. Drop the batter from a tablespoon onto wax paper. Keep refrigerated. Makes about 36 cookies.

Lucille Le Lievre
St. Joseph du Maine, N.S.

Cape Breton Highlands
National Park

Ginger Krinkles

¾ cup	vegetable oil	175 mL
1	egg	1
1 cup	white sugar	250 mL
¼ cup	molasses	50 mL
2 cups	flour, sifted	500 mL
½ tsp.	salt	2 mL
2 tsp.	baking soda	10 mL
1½ tsp.	cinnamon	7 mL
1½ tsp.	ginger	7 mL

Combine vegetable oil, egg, sugar, and molasses. Beat well.

Sift together flour, salt, baking soda, cinnamon, and ginger. Add to sugar mixture.

Roll dough into small balls. Place them on ungreased cookie sheets, 3" (7 cm) apart. Dip a glass in sugar and use it to flatten the balls. Keep the glass covered with sugar so that it won't stick to the cookies. Bake for 8-10 minutes at 350°F (180°C). Makes about 5 dozen.

Roxie Ennes
Onanole, Man.

Riding Mountain
National Park

In the early days of the "the old campground", at Clear Lake, people used to heat stones and place them in their beds before retiring. The stones served as very effective bed warmers!

See photograph page 128.

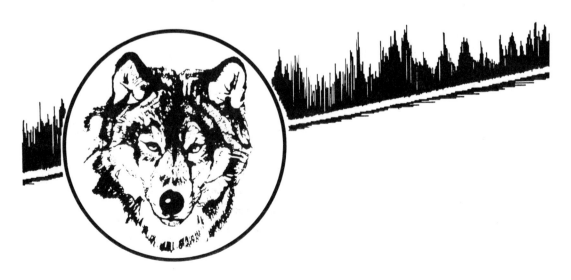

Blanche's Peanut Butter
Chocolate Chip Cookies

½ cup	margarine	125 mL
½ cup	brown sugar	125 mL
½ cup	white sugar	125 mL
1	egg	1
½ tsp.	vanilla	2 mL
1 cup	crunchy peanut butter	250 mL
1½ cups	flour	375 mL
½ tsp.	salt	2 mL
½ tsp.	baking soda	2 mL
1 cup	chocolate chips	250 mL

Cream margarine and sugars. Add egg, vanilla, and peanut butter, beat well.

Sift together flour, salt, and baking soda. Add to creamed ingredients and mix well. Add chocolate chips.

Roll into 1" (2.5 cm) balls. Place them on ungreased cookie sheets and press flat with a fork. Bake for about 10-12 minutes at 375°F (190°C). Makes approximately 5 dozen cookies.

Blanche and Hazel Tweedie
Kouchibouguac Village, N.B.

Kouchibouguac
National park

Blanche and Hazel Tweedie, two sisters who are well past retirement age, live together in a large stone house in the village of Kouchibouguac. The house was constructed in 1823 as a stage house for weary travellers. Several times a month, Blanche and Hazel will prepare a large "Man-Size Meal" and invite several weary park managers over to a feast of good food. Those who cannot attend or who are not invited are rewarded with several bags of cookies, fudge, and doughnuts.

See photograph page 128.

Butterscotch Squares

¼ cup	butter	50 mL
1 cup	brown sugar	250 mL
1	egg	1
¾ cup	flour	175 mL
1 tsp.	baking powder	5 mL
1½ tsp.	vanilla	7 mL
½ cup	chopped nuts	125 mL

In a large saucepan, melt butter and sugar but don't cook. Cool slightly, add the egg. Beat well. Add remaining ingredients and mix well. Pour into a greased 8" x 8" (20 cm x 20 cm) baking pan. Bake 15-20 minutes at 350°F (180°C). Ice with Light Butter Icing (recipe follows). Serves 16.

Betty Rose
Summerland, B.C.

Riding Mountain
National Park

Light Butter Icing

¾ cup	icing sugar	175 mL
½ cup	butter	125 mL
½ tsp.	vanilla	2 mL
¼ cup	light cream	50 mL
¼ cup	boiling water	50 mL

Blend sugar and butter well, using high speed with electric beaters. Add vanilla. Add cream, a little at a time, beating after each addition.

Add boiling water, a teaspoon at a time, beating after each addition. It is very important to add the cream and the water a little bit at a time, beating between each addition or the icing will not be smooth and creamy. This is a light delicious icing.

Betty Rose
Summerland, B.C.

Riding Mountain
National Park

See photograph page 128.

Kejimkujik National Park
Nova Scotia

Deep in the backwoods, there is a land of meandering, drifting waters that invites you to wander and explore. The Mic Mac Indians were the first to accept the invitation of these abundant lakes connected by flowing rivers. These waters served as canoe routes in their seasonal home. This nomadic tribe fished and hunted in these depths, portaging and camping in its stillness. Many of the lakes still bear Mic Mac names. In the early eighteen hundreds, the Mic Macs almost disappeared as the Europeans followed the call of these water routes. The settlers later used the river system to float logs downstream to saw mills and towns.

About a century ago, another use of the waters began. The Kejimkujik area was renowned for its excellent trout fishing and moose hunting. Local people began to act as guides, taking sportsmen back into the country by canoe. These guides followed the traditional canoe routes and portages and camped in many of the same places that the Mic Macs used for centuries. Gradually, a number of lodges and resorts were established to cater to sportsmen. Over the years, these resorts saw a change in clientel until, eventually, families were coming to enjoy a summer vacation in the wilds. Canoeing and the enjoyment of the peaceful surroundings were most important, however, trout fishing remained popular.

Even the name Kejimkujik reinforces the significance of the waterways. Kejimkujik is the officially adopted spelling of the Mic Mac word. The meaning of the word is still not precisely clear. Kejimkujik was first stated by Rev. Silas Rand as meaning "Swelling Parts". This could refer to the large lake with small rivers entering and leaving. Others believe it is connected to the flooding or water level changes with the seasons and the construction of eel weirs. More recently, it has been suggested that Rev. Rand was politely censoring the source of the meaning "Swelled Parts" which really referred to the effect upon the men of labouring hard to canoe across the large lake. Whatever the meaning, Kejimkujik certainly describes it more poetically!

Today, the park offers the same enticing invitation of this water labyrinth. You can melt into the landscape as you follow the same, centuries old, canoe routes and view life from a river perspective as you float stealthily by. Nothing compares with the isolation of a secluded island haven or the comforting call of a loon or owl as you gather around the campfire, succumbing to the exhaustion of a vigorous canoeing trek. For centuries, these same experiences have enticed people to the land of Kejimkujik!

Smartie Cookies

1 cup	sugar	250 mL
1 cup	brown sugar	250 mL
½ cup	butter	125 mL
½ cup	peanut butter	125 mL
3	eggs	3
1 tbsp.	corn syrup	15 mL
½ tsp.	vanilla	2 mL
2 tbsp.	baking soda	30 mL
4½ cups	oatmeal	1.125 mL
½ cup	chocolate chips	125 mL
½ cup	Smarties	125 mL

Cream sugar, brown sugar, butter, and peanut butter. Add eggs, corn syrup, vanilla, and baking soda and mix well. Add oatmeal and chocolate, mix thoroughly. Form dough into small balls. Place on greased cookie sheets, press a Smartie into each cookie. Bake 12 minutes at 350°C (180°C). Makes 3-4 dozen.

Olga Muller Friesen
Winnipeg, Man.

Riding Mountain
National Park

See photograph page 128.

Buttermilk Fudge

1 cup	buttermilk	250 mL
2 cups	white sugar	500 mL
1 tsp.	baking soda	5 mL
2 cups	pecan halves or chopped walnuts	500 mL
1 tsp.	vanilla	5 mL
1 tbsp.	butter	15 mL

Combine buttermilk, sugar, and soda in a large saucepan, stir until sugar is dissolved. Cook over low to medium heat. Stir constantly and boil mixture until it reaches the soft-ball stage. (Drop a small amount into cold water. If you can form the syrup into a soft ball with your fingers, it is ready.)

Remove saucepan from heat. Add nuts, vanilla, and butter. Beat briskly until it starts to get thick. Spoon fudge out onto waxed paper and allow to cool before removing the paper. Makes approximately 12-16 pieces of fudge.

Emmet Martin
P.E.I.

P.E.I.
National Park

Chocolate Torte

1 cup	flour	250 mL
½ cup	butter	125 mL
1 tsp.	sugar	5 mL
½ cup	chopped nuts	125 mL
8 oz.	cream cheese	250 g
1 cup	icing sugar	250 mL
16 oz.	container Cool Whip	500 mL
6 oz.	pkg. instant chocolate pudding	170 g
6 oz.	pkg. instant vanilla pudding	170 g
2 cups	milk	500 mL
16 oz.	container Cool Whip	500 mL
	or	
2 cups	whipped cream	500 mL

Combine flour and sugar. Cut in butter with pastry blender. Add chopped nuts. Pat into a 9" x 13" (23 cm x 33 cm) pan. Bake 15-20 minutes at 350°F (180°C) until lightly brown. Cool.

2nd layer: Beat cream cheese and icing sugar. Gently fold in Cool Whip. Pour this over crust.

3rd layer: Combine the pudding mixes and milk. Heat in the top of a double boiler about 3-5 minutes until thick. Cool this mixture and pour over cheese layer.

4th layer: Spread Cool Whip or whipped cream over pudding layer. Decorate with shaved chocolate. Store in refrigerator. Serves 20.

Beverly Rutherford
Field, B.C.

Yoho
National Park

Beverly and her husband have spent 22 years in Yoho National Park. They raised their 2 daughters in the park and her husband is now Chief Park Warden of this National Park.

See photograph page 128.

Rolled Oats Shortbread

1½ cups	flour	375 mL
1 cup	brown sugar	250 mL
½ tsp.	salt	2 mL
1 tsp.	baking soda	5 mL
2 cups	rolled oats	500 mL
1 cup	melted margarine	250 mL
½ tsp.	vanilla	2 mL

Preheat oven to 350°F (180°C). While heating oven, melt the margarine (in the oven) in a 10" x 12" (25 cm x 30 cm) pan.

Crumble dry ingredients with fingers. Add melted margarine and vanilla and mix well. Press flat in the greasy pan. Bake about 12 minutes at 350°F (180°C). Cut into squares while still warm. This is a quick and easy snack. Serves 16-20.

Charlotte Stewart
Surrey, B.C.

Riding Mountain
National Park

Strawberry Squares

2½ cups	graham wafer crumbs	625 mL
½ cup	melted butter	125 mL
1 cup	boiling water	250 mL
1 tbsp.	envelope unflavoured gelatin	30 mL
3 oz.	pkg. strawberry Jell-o	85 g
2 cups	fresh strawberries, sliced or whole frozen strawberries	500 mL
3 oz.	pkg. Dream Whip	85 g

Combine graham wafer crumbs and melted butter. Press firmly into the bottom of an 8" x 8" (20 cm x 20 cm) or 9" x 9" (23 cm x 23 cm) pan. Bake for 5 minutes at 375°F (190°C). Cool thoroughly.

Combine boiling water, gelatin, Jell-o, and strawberries in a saucepan. Bring to a boil. Place in the refrigerator, and chill until it begins to thicken. Spoon over crust.

Prepare Dream Whip according to package direction. Spread over strawberry layer. Serves 8-10.

Karen MacKenzie
Norris Point, Nfld.

Gros Morne
National Park

See photograph page 128.

Cape Breton Highlands National Park

Nova Scotia

Step back into the past and discover the exhilaration of John Cabot as he penetrated a new land. Marvel at the diversity that greeted him as he stepped into the New World.

As you wind your way along the world famous Cabot Trail, the spectacular scenery and variation enthralls you, as the trail hugs the coastline, climbs the highlands and wanders through valleys. The park is a huge plain that was lifted above the sea eons ago. This plateau is covered with vast bogs, dry barrens, small ponds, and lakes. In contrast to the plateau, are the deep valleys that have been cut into the tableland by rivers and streams. Superb waterfalls triumph where stubborn rock has failed to succumb to its forces. The river valleys succour maples, beech, and ash while the park's highest arctic-like elevations are mournfully barren. The park's west coast borders the Gulf of St. Lawrence and boasts the drama of its steep cliffs. The Atlantic Ocean, to the east, borders a coast of rocky headlands and sandy beaches.

Variation characterized the settlement of the area. Portuguese settled in the vicinity of Ingonish in the 1520's. This later became the second largest centre on the island. During the 17th century, the French occupied Cape Breton Island, then known as "Isle Royale". The expulsion of the Acadians from mainland Nova Scotia prompted the establishment of French settlements along Cape Breton's western shore. This began a diversity of settlements — Acadians settled in Cheticamp, Scots in Pleasant Bay and Cape North, Newfoundlanders in Neil's Harbour and a blend of Irish and Scots in Ingonish.

The common ground for the settlers was their love of seafood. The variety is overwhelming. Each spring, people eagerly await their first feed of lobster. After the lobster season finishes, the crab and swordfish seasons soon begin. The swordfish are caught by harpoon as they sun themselves at the surface of the water. Some of them weigh up to 250 kg and provide a sumptuous barbecue treat. Codfish, haddock, flounder, halibut, and mackeral appear regularly on local menus. When the winter storms arrive, the fishermen haul their boats ashore and the communities resign themselves to eating like the unfortunates in the rest of Canada!

So, whether you taste the bounty of the coast or savour the grandeur of the natural surroundings, Cape Breton Highlands National Park is an experience of diversity, not soon forgotten.

Opera Roll

3 cups	white sugar	750 mL
⅔ cup	white corn syrup	150 mL
¾ cup	boiling water	175 mL
2	egg whites	2
½ tsp.	vanilla	2 mL
1 cup	icing sugar	250 mL
14 oz.	can sweetened condensed milk	398 mL
½ cup	margarine	125 mL
6 tbsp.	dark corn syrup	90 mL
1 cup	nuts, chopped, walnuts or pecans	250 mL

Combine sugar, corn syrup, and boiling water in a large saucepan. Heat slowly to boiling point. Stir until the sugar is dissolved. Boil until the firm hard-ball stage, 250°F (120°C). Cool slightly.

Beat egg whites until stiff. Gradually add syrup mixture and continue beating until thickened. Add vanilla. Form into logs approximately 1" (2.5 cm) in diameter, and 4" (10 cm) long. Roll each log in icing sugar and then set aside.

Combine sweetened condensed milk, margarine, and corn syrup in a large frying pan or large shallow vessel. Stir constantly and boil to the hard ball stage. Roll each log in the toffee mixture and then roll in chopped nuts. Makes approximately 2 or 3 rolls.

Gale Robinson
Winnipeg, Man.

Riding Mountain
National Park

Fruit Balls

½ lb.	figs	250 g
½ lb.	raisins	250 g
½ lb.	dates	250 g
¼ lb.	cherries	115 g
¼ lb.	peel	115 g
½ lb.	walnuts	250 g

Grind all ingredients, with a food grinder or a food processor.

Mix well and form into 1" (2.5 cm) balls. Roll each ball in sugar. Store in the refrigerator. Makes about 45 balls.

Karen Townsend
Albert, N.B.

Fundy
National Park

See photograph page 128.

CHILDREN'S FAVOURITES
&
OUTDOOR TREATS

Peanut Butter Balls

1 cup	peanut butter	250 mL
1 cup	icing sugar	250 mL
4 tbsp.	butter	60 mL
¼ cup	nuts, chopped	50 mL
¼ cup	rice krispies	50 mL
3 squares	semisweet chocolate	3 squares
3 tbsp.	butter	45 mL
1	1″ (2.5 cm) square paraffin wax	1

Combine the peanut butter, icing sugar, butter, chopped nuts, and rice krispies. Drop the mixture from a teaspoon onto a floured board. Coat the batter with flour and roll it in your hands until it forms a ball.

Place the balls on a cookie sheet. Freeze for several hours.

Melt the chocolate, butter, and paraffin in wax in the top of a double boiler. Use 2 forks to dip the peanut butter balls in the melted chocolate. Cover a cookie sheet with wax paper and place the chocolate covered balls on the wax paper. Return the balls to the freezer. Place in the refrigerator for about ½ hour before serving. Makes 2½ dozen.

Sandra Morrison
Chicken Delight Restaurant, Wasagaming, Man.

Riding Mountain
National Park

See photograph page 128.

Lemon Cubes

5-6	fresh lemons	5-6
1	glass of water	1
2-3 tbsp.	sugar	30-45 mL

Squeeze the juice from the lemons. Pour the juice into ice cube containers and freeze.

To make lemonade, put 2 frozen lemon ice cubes into a glass of water. Add 2-3 tbsp. sugar, to suit your taste. Stir well. As the ice cubes melt — you get lemonade! Makes 4 to 6 glasses of lemonade.

Andrew Mense
Age 7

Riding Mountain
National Park

Gros Morne National Park

Newfoundland

Join this journey towards the centre of the earth and back through time. Gros Morne National Park offers an interesting combination of the two.

The journey towards the centre of the earth begins at the tablelands. They are made of peridotite, a rock that is found in the mantle of the earth. The mantle is a dense but active layer deep below the earth's surface. This land gradually rose from the mysterious depths of the sea and is still rising. Plant life struggles to establish a foothold in this foreign rock. Having been forced up from the earth's interior, peridotite has an unusual chemical composition with high concentrations of poisonous elements. Thus life is sparse, giving these overpowering and conspicuous tablelands an isolated, eerie atmosphere.

From the depths of the earth, you are transported through time, you have the opportunity to see layer upon layer of geological history unfold before your eyes. In the cliffs near Green Cove, the characteristic fossils from different geological periods are meticuloulsy layered one on top of the other, tangibly portraying the earth's evoluntionary history.

Another ancient story is recounted by the Cow Head Braccias. Encased in rock, side by side, are fossils of animals that lived in shallow warm seas, together with fossils of creatures that survived only in the icy depths. The explanation is that long ago, some of these rocks were a part of the edge of the shallow shelf of the continent that stretched into the sea. The shelf would fall avalanche-style into the dark depths, entrapping the animals eternally with it. These are compacted with the other aquatic life in the other ocean debris and eventually raised to the surface to reveal their story.

The past reaches out to us with evidence of three pre-European cultures. As early as 2500 B.C. Maritime Archaic Indians depended on the marine mammals and the caribou in the region for their survival. The more advanced Dorcet Eskimos used better refined knife blades, projectile points, and harpoons to more successfully hunt the same wildlife. Later, the Beothuk Indians established residence in the area about 800 A.D., harvesting the sea in the summer and following the caribou herds inland during winter. The Beothuks, sadly, became extinct in 1829 with the lonely death of Shanadithit, the last member of this proud race.

The past constantly emerges to recite its multifaceted history as you journey through this timeless corner of the earth.

Cheese Balls

4 tbsp.	crushed pineapple	60 mL
10	maraschino cherries, cut into small pieces	10
8 oz.	cream cheese (softened)	250 g
½ cup	sugar	125 mL
½ cup	dessicated coconut	125 mL
⅛ tsp.	salt	0.5 mL
14	graham wafers, crushed finely	14
1 tbsp.	butter, melted	15 mL
1 tsp.	sugar	5 mL

Drain the pineapple and cherries very well on paper towels. Combine them with the cream cheese, ½ cup (125 mL) sugar, coconut, and salt. Mix well and chill in the refrigerator.

Combine wafer crumbs, melted butter, and sugar. Roll the chilled mixture into small balls. Roll the balls in wafer mixture. Freeze immediately. Place balls in the refrigerator for about ½ hour before serving time. Makes 2-3 dozen.

Mrs. Davidson
Winnipeg, Man.

Riding Mountain
National Park

See photograph page 128.

Orange Cookies

½ cup	margarine	125 mL
¾ cup	sugar	175 mL
1	egg, slightly beaten	1
½ tsp.	orange juice	2 mL
1½ cups	flour	375 mL
1½ tsp.	baking powder	7 mL
	the grated rind of 1 orange	

Cream the margarine. Add sugar and blend well. Add beaten egg and orange juice.

Combine the flour and baking powder. Add to the creamed mixture and stir in grated orange rind.

Drop from a teaspoon onto a greased cookie sheet. Bake for 8-10 minutes at 350°F (180°C). Makes about 50-60 cookies.

Ryan & Cheryl Ffrench
Age 5; Age 7

Pacific Rim
National Park

Yogurt Dessert

2 cups	flavoured yogurt	500 mL
	granola	
	chopped nuts	
	shaved chocolate	

Spoon the yogurt into 4 dishes. Put the granola, chopped nuts, and shaved chocolate into separate dishes. Then let everyone decorate their own dessert! You can also use cherries, dried fruit, bananas, mandarin orange segments, or anything you like for toppings.

Sarah-Jane & Christopher Oldham
Age 9; Age 6

Georgian Bay Islands
National Park

Banana Apple Fluff

1	banana	1
1 tbsp.	apple juice	15 mL
¾ cups	apple sauce	175 mL
2 cups	whipping cream, whipped	500 mL
½ cup	plain yogurt	125 mL
¾ cup	rice krispies or any crunchy cereal	175 mL
½ tsp.	cinnamon	2 mL
½ cup	chopped nuts	125 mL
	shaved chocolate	

Mash the banana with the apple juice, by hand or in a blender. Add apple sauce (homemade is nice but not necessary), whipped cream, and yogurt. Refrigerate.

Process rice krispies in a blender to make crumbs. Add cinnamon.

Serve Fluff in dishes. Put the rice krispie mixture, nuts, and shaved chocolate in small bowls. Let everyone make their own topping! Serves 4.

Cara & Lise Brown
Age 10; Age 6

Prince Albert
National Park

Pocket Stew

¼ cup	ground beef	50 mL
¼ cup	peas	50 mL
¼ cup	sliced carrots	50 mL
¼ cup	diced potatoes	50 mL
	salt	
	pepper	
2	pieces of tin foil	2

Lay a 10" (25 cm) square of tin foil, shiny side up, on a table. Put the ground beef, peas, carrots, and potatoes on the foil. Sprinkle with salt and pepper.

Lift 2 opposite sides of the tin foil up until they meet. Fold the edges together until they are sealed tightly. Fold the other two sides up to seal tightly.

Place the other piece of tin foil, shiny side up, on the table Turn the stew package upside down on top of the foil and seal in the same way as you did before.

Bake on the coals of an open fire or barbecue for 10-15 minutes, until done. Makes stew for 1.

Camp Wannakumbac
Clear Lake, Man.

During the summer months, the Riding Mountain Conference Centre operates the Camp Wannakumbac summer camping program for young people. Since the centre is just outside the boundary of Riding Mountain National Park, children throughout the years have participated in activities which have been in keeping with the philosophy and surroundings of the park.

How to Make a Quinzee

lots of snow
some shovels

Make a large pile of snow, about 4 or 5' (1-1.5 m) high. (We have seen some 6' (2 m) high.) Let the snow pile sit for 2 or 3 days. Use smaller shovels to hollow out a hole for the door and then gradually hollow out the inside to form a winter house. This is a good family project and provides hours of fun for children!

Celes Davar
Wasagaming, Man.

Riding Mountain
National Park

Terra Nova National Park

Newfoundland

Your first impression of Terra Nova National Park conjures up images of the furious North Atlantic slamming passionately into unyielding headlands and massive swells pounding the decks of fragile fishing boats. The ominous boreal forest inspires visions of harsh, deep, mysterious woods and oozing bogs. But, the true nature of this fjord-pierced, island-studded coastline is peaceful co-existence as the Boreal landscape touches sheltered seas. From this quiet harmony, you can discover the leviathans of the coast.

The first mammoth of the deep is, of course, the surreptitious bulk of the pilot whale. Affectionately called "the pothead" it has been adopted as the symbol for park interpretive activities. Man's affinity for these elusive creatures is tantalized as they perform teasingly before your watchful eyes. Also vying for attention are the agile and theatrical dolphins jumping and leaping in merriment.

Disguised in the dazzling solitary splendour of a shivering sculpture is the ominous presence of the iceberg! Although its frosty green-blue crown challenges the most artistic craftsperson, these majestic chunks of ice can be deadly! These deceivers conceal their magnitude in the icy fathoms with almost nine-tenths of their volume being underwater. If they are approached too closely, they can cunningly break-up or turn, to create a disasterous whirlpool of suction. These fantasy monoliths break free from the lips of their parent glaciers, tumble anxiously into the freedom of the sea and float gracefully south. Rock particles ground into the glacial ice give the icebergs their shimmering, ethereal colour tones. Eventually, their magnificent artistry sadly melts, adding its fresh water, thousands of years old, to the salty waters of Bona Vista Bay.

In bygone days, one of the feared marauders of the deep was the pirate ships which terrorized seagoing vessels and coastal villages. One of the most famous pirates in this area was the notorious Peter Easton. This swashbuckling pirate sailed along the eastern coast of Newfoundland destroying property and ships as he swept supremely by. Easton never suffered for his crimes. Instead, he lived happily ever after, bought a castle, married a princess and lived an extravagent life off the spoils of his spine-tingling escapades.

These leviathans of past and present do not threaten modern Newfoundlanders. Their dearly beloved sea shanties and treasured lore echoes proudly and exuberantly in this lush and peaceful land that touches the serenity of the sea.

Maple Baked Beans

1½ cups	large dry lima beans	375 mL
1½ cups	dry kidney beans	375 mL
2 quarts	water	2 L
1 tsp.	salt	5 mL
½ lb.	smoked bacon ends	250 g
2	bay leaves	2
3	onions, chopped	3
½ cup	pure maple syrup	125 mL
4 tbsp.	tomato paste	60 mL
¾ cup	bean water	175 mL

Soak lima beans and kidney beans separately, overnight, in 1 quart (1 L) of water for each batch. In the morning, add fresh water to cover, and ½ tsp. (2 mL) salt to each batch. Bring to a boil, separately, and cover. Reduce heat and simmer until beans are barely tender. Drain beans and reserve the liquid.

Place bacon chunks into heavy casserole. Add beans, bay leaves, onions, and syrup. Stir until smooth and add to bean pot. Pour in enough bean liquid to just cover the beans.

Bake, covered, for 5 or 6 hours at 275°F (140°C) or until beans are very tender. If necessary, add additional reserved bean liquid to keep the beans moist during cooking. Taste for seasoning. Add salt and pepper or a few drops of maple flavouring. The flavour improves with reheating. Serves 6-8.

Duane West
Alma, N.B.

Fundy
National Park

Campfire Potatoes

5-6	medium potatoes, sliced	5-6
1	onion, sliced	1
¼ cup	butter or margarine	50 mL
3	slices processed cheese, cut in squares	3
	sliced carrots (if desired)	

Spread the potatoes, onions, and carrots on foil wrap. Top with the butter and cheese. Close the foil tightly around the vegetables and bake over a fire or barbecue for 45 minutes, turning frequently. Serves 5-6.

Mike and Joanne Murphy
Edmonton, Alta.

Riding Mountain
National Park

Chocolate Bananas

| 1 | ripe banana | 1 |
| 1 | chocolate bar | 1 |

Lay a ripe banana on its side and peel back about ½" (1.3 cm) width of skin — but do not pull the skin right off.

With a knife, cut a trough in the banana for its full length. Save the wedge of banana. Press small pieces of chocolate into the trough and then replace the wedge of banana. Put the skin back into place.

Wrap the banana in a layer of tin foil and lay it in the campfire embers for 10-15 minutes. The banana will become quite soft and impregnated with chocolate. Eat with a spoon.

For variation, sprinkle cinnamon over the banana wedge or replace the wedge with pieces of marshmallow. Serves 1.

Bernie Lieff
Waterton Park, Alta.

Waterton Lakes
National Park

Bernie learned of this campfire dessert treat from his scoutmaster, who said it was popular with the men he served with in the Army while stationed in India many years ago.

If you bring eggs, it's a good idea to break them into a sealable plastic container and pack that. Or, put unbroken eggs in a pack of oatmeal, if they do break the oatmeal will seal them up.

Don't forget that popcorn makes a nice nighttime snack to cook over the fire.

Kejimkujik
National Park

Laminaria Stew

1	young laminaria plant (about 2' (60 cm) long)	1
½ lb.	pork chops	500 g
2 cups	water	500 mL
2 tsp.	salt	10 mL
2 tbsp.	soy sauce	30 mL

Wash the laminaria plant. Cut the blade portion into strips about ½" (1.3 cm) wide. Set aside.

Chop pork chops into cubes about ½" x 1" (1.3 cm x 2.5 cm). In a large frying pan, bring water to a boil. Add pork, salt, and soy sauce. Boil for 15 minutes. Add laminaria strips and cook an additional 10 minutes. Serves 2.

The Park Interpreters   *Prince Edward Island*
National Park

Laminaria is a species of oarweed. In the Bay of Fundy region, it can attain a length of 30 feet or more between the months of March and July.

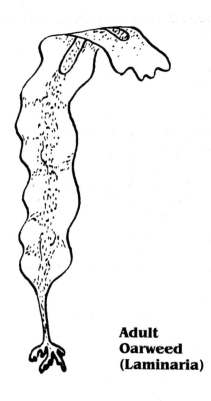

**Adult
Oarweed
(Laminaria)**

Grassland National Park

Saskatchewan

Canada's newest national park is a tribute to the prairie. At a quick glance, the prairies are often dismissed as a flat "nothingness" that connect Ontario and British Columbia. However, there is a rare beauty here, that slowly unfolds before a patient observer. The subtle colours, tones, and moods of the prairie, as well as the soft reliefs in twilight, and the sweet smell of prairie grass is captured forever in the time warp of Grasslands National Park.

You can step back into the past and experience the original grandeur and solitude that greeted early explorers. When the park begins to operate a full program, it will present reminders of a prairie past. Remnant teepee rings are memories of the Plains Indians who associated themselves with a partricular herd of buffalo. Following their herd to this summer range, they placed rocks around their tents to anchor them. When the buffalo moved on, the homes were dismantled and the rocks were left behind in their teepee ring formations.

History took us further back when Sir George Mercier Dawson made the first recorded discovery of dinosaur remains in 1874 in the Kildeer Badlands. These badlands are aptly named because they are difficult to travel and impossible to farm. The badlands continually change because their lack of vegetation makes them susceptible to erosion. Water, their worst enemy, in the form of rain, run-off, hail, and sleet, carves eerie peaks, pinnacles, conspicuous isolated hills known as buttes, and raised surfaces called turtlebacks.

The most important element is the grasslands which provide a home for the black-tailed prairie dog which appears nowhere else in Canada. Grasslands National Park contains dozens of species of grasses which all have a tenacity and a capacity to survive. For this survival, grasses have hollow stems strengthened by solid nodes allowing them to bend in the prairie winds without breaking. This hardy species has an extensive root system and can absorb moisture from the slightest shower. A blade of grass grows from its base so that it recovers from grazing and rebounds quickly after fires. This was one of the keys to its abundance because the Indians frequently set the prairies ablaze while hunting and during warfare. The shrubs and trees succumbed to these disasters and the solidly based grasses dominated.

Just as the grasses have braved the prairie elements, survived and flourished, so too have many settlers who came to call this vast expanse home. It is in the context of these rolling grasslands that many Canadians have found their roots!

Backwoods Bannock

Every backwoods spudfighter (camp cook for the uninitiated) has their own time-tested recipe for that staple item of campfood — bannock. Its preparation requires no special skill or appliance — the more primitive, the better.

ENRICHED BANNOCK

3 cups	white flour	750 mL
2 cups	whole-wheat flour	500 mL
1 cup	powdered milk	250 mL
6 tbsp.	sugar	90 mL
2 tbsp.	baking powder	30 mL
⅛ tsp.	salt	0.5 mL
½ cup	water	125 mL

Combine all the ingredients and mix well. Add enough water to make a soft dough. Mix and knead to a bread dough consistency.

Grease a large cast-iron frying pan and place over an open fire. Form bannock dough into a circle the size of the frying pan. Cook until golden brown.

BASIC BANNOCK

4½ cups	flour	1.125 L
6 tbsp.	sugar	90 mL
2 tbsp.	baking powder	30 mL
⅛ tsp.	salt	0.5 mL
1 tsp.	lard, melted or vegetable oil	5 mL
½ cup	water	125 mL

Follow instructions for Enriched Bannock.

The best bannock only begins with these basic ingredients. That real woodsy flavour is a product of slow cooking in a frying pan over the campfire and the smattering of ashes, insects, soil and grass that find their way into the dough. These extra ingredients together with the company of friends and family among the forests of our National Parks make for the most flavourful bannock. Enjoy!

Brad Muir
Waskesiu Lake, Sask.

Prince Albert
National Park

Bannock Delight

EQUIPMENT

1	small pan
1	wooden stick, 3' (1 m) long and about 1" (2 cm) in diameter sharpened on one end. (Cut the stick outside the park!)

INGREDIENTS

DELIGHT

2 cups	fresh berries (blueberries)	500 mL
⅓ cup	brown sugar	75 mL
1 tsp.	brandy	5 mL

In a saucepan, squash the berries with a fork. Add sugar and brandy. Simmer over low heat until thick.

BANNOCK

2 cups	flour	500 mL
2 tbsp.	sugar	30 mL
2 tsp.	baking powder	10 mL
⅛ cm	salt	0.5 mL
2 tbsp.	lard	30 mL
¼ cup	water	50 mL
	butter	

Combine dry ingredients. Work in the lard until mealy. Add enough cold water to form a dough. Form the dough around the sharp end of the wooden stick until you have a cone about 6" (15 cm) long and 1" (2 cm) thick.

Cook over an open fire, turning frequently, until golden brown. When cooked, the bannock will slide off the stick easily.

Melt a slab of butter in the bannock cone and fill with the delight.

CAUTION

If the fire is too hot or you drink too much brandy, the bannock may turn black, which means that you have burned it. In this case, pour the delight directly on the stick and eat the stick!

Paul Galbraith
Bonne Bay, Nfld.

Gros Morne
National Park

Super Granola

1 cup	raw wheat germ	250 mL
4-5 cups	rolled oats	1 - 1.25 L
¾ cup	walnuts, chopped	175 mL
½ cup	sesame seeds	125 mL
½ cup	sunflower seeds, shelled	125 mL
½ cup	unsweetened coconut	125 mL
¼ cup	brown or demerara sugar	50 mL
½ tsp.	salt	2 mL
¾ cup	vegetable oil	175 mL
½ cup	water	125 mL
½ cup	honey	125 mL
1½ tsp.	vanilla	7 mL
1 cup	raisins or dried fruit	250 mL

Combine dry ingredients in a large bowl. Combine vegetable oil, water, honey, and vanilla in blender. Pour over dry ingredients and mix well.

Place granola on 2 - 10½" x 15" (26 cm x 37 cm) baking sheets. Bake for about 20-25 minutes at 300°F (150°C). Stir the granola approximately every 5 minutes. Granola is done when it is golden brown. Cool and add dried fruit.

Store in airtight containers in a cool dry place. Serve as a cereal with milk, as a dry snack, or sprinkle on yogurt or ice cream. Makes approximately 10 cups.

Claudette Saquet
Wasagaming, Man.

Riding Mountain
National Park

See photograph page 16.

Gorp

2 cups	coconut	500 mL
2 cups	peanuts	500 mL
2 cups	raisins	500 mL
2 cups	chocolate chips	500 mL
2 cups	rolled oats, uncooked	500 mL
2 cups	sunflower seeds	500 mL
2 cups	sesame seeds	500 mL

Combine all the ingredients and mix well. Add more dried fruit if desired. This snack is perfect for the trail.

Kejimkujik
National Park

For Want of Water

When the boundary for Kejimkujik National Park was first cut out and marked the Park Superintendent requested the Warden Service to check it. To do this, a group of Wardens had to walk the route in the middle of a hot dry summer.

Now Kejimkujik has so many rivers and lakes, that it is about one-third fresh water. While there are no lakes right on the boundary, it is crossed by many small streams. So it was that the Wardens carried little or no water with them. It didn't take them long to realize their error. With the heat of summer, most small streams were completely dry and despite hours of walking in the hot sun, no water could be found.

Finally in desperation, in the middle of another dry bog, the Wardens were forced to drink the water from the leaves of pitcher plants. One wonders if that famous line was repeated, "Hey there's a fly in my water."

Kejimkujik
National Park

Sportsman's Delight

trout
potatoes, cubed
onions, diced
butter
salt, pepper
milk

Brown the onion in butter. Add water, potatoes, salt and pepper to taste. While the potatoes are cooking, boil the trout in a separate pot until done. Remove skin and bones from the trout and flake into pieces. Add trout pieces to the potato mixture and simmer. Add milk and continue to simmer, being careful not to boil.

This trout chowder recipe was cooked in pots over an open fire by one of the early guides in the area. The quantities will vary according to personal preference and the size of the group.

Kejimkujik
National Park

Falaise á la Mauricienne

(The Cliffs of La Mauricie)

This recipe has been used in the interpretive program at La Mauricie National Park for several year to explain the geology of the area in simple terms.

In a large pan (several km square), layer mud, sand, limestone and other chopped stone. Lava flows can be used to add colour.

Dig a hole 30 km deep and put the dirt aside. Place the pan at the bottom of the hole, cover it up again and set a timer for about 50 million years. At the end of this time, do not remove it from the hole but gradually remove the covering material for the next 400 million years. When it comes to the surface, sharpen a glacier and slice. Makes enough for all visitors to enjoy.

Luckily, a cook 1 billion years ago made plenty of this delicacy for us to enjoy for a long time to come!

Mryka Hall-Beyer
Scotstown, Qué.

La Mauricie
National Park

Truite à la Wapizagonke
(Wapizagonke Trout)

Even though this dish can be baked in an oven, it is also a delectable treat during a canoe or camping trip.

Hurry to catch your first few trouts (naturally of a good size)! Place the fish in aluminum foil. Add butter, salt, pepper, and chopped onions. Pour white wine over top. Wrap securely and tightly with foil. Place the package on the fire's embers or in the oven for approximately 10-15 minutes. (Cooking time will vary depending upon the size of the trout.)

Serve on a bed of rice or couscous, along with a glass of wine. Savour this dish while you are listening to the loon's call.

Bernard Jolicoeur
Ste. Foy, Qué.

La Mauricie
National Park

Truite á La Wapizagonke (Truite En Papillotte)

Bien que ce plat puisse être prépare au four, il est surtout conçu pour être dégusté et canot-camping. On prépare le bagage de canot-camping suffisamment léger pour pouvoir se permettre de trainer l'excés de poids que représentent un oignon et une bouteille de vin.

On s'empresse de capturer quelques truites de belle taille. On place les truites dans us grand morceau de papier d'aluminium, On met un peu de beurre, de sel, de poivre et d'oignon haché. On verse un peu de vin blanc sur le tout. On referme le papier d'1aluminiun pour en faire une papillotte géante le plus étanche possible. On met le tout sur la braise ou au four selon le cas environ 10 à 15 minutes (selon la grosseur des truites).

En camping, on peut servir sur lit de riz ou de couscous. On verse ensuite un verre de vin blanc à sa compagnie et on savoure le tout en écoutant le chant des huarts.

Bernard Jolicoeur
Ste. Foy, Qué.

La Mauricie
National Park

Index

187

Index of National Park Descriptions

A GIFT TO REMEMBER
PARKLAND PALATE
c/o ARK Publishing
697 Patricia Avenue
Winnipeg, Manitoba, Canada
R3T 3A8

Please send me _____copies of "**PARKLAND PALATE**" @ $12.95 each plus $1.50 <u>each</u> postage and handling.

Amount enclosed $ _____ plus postage and handling $ _____

Total enclosed $ _____

Name _____

City _____Province/State _____

Postal Code/Zip _____

Make cheque payable to ARK Publishing.

....

A GIFT TO REMEMBER
PARKLAND PALATE
c/o ARK Publishing
697 Patricia Avenue
Winnipeg, Manitoba, Canada
R3T 3A8

Please send me _____copies of "**PARKLAND PALATE**" @ $12.95 each plus $1.50 <u>each</u> postage and handling.

Amount enclosed $ _____ plus postage and handling $ _____

Total enclosed $ _____

Name _____

City _____Province/State _____

Postal Code/Zip _____

Make cheque payable to ARK Publishing.